This book is dedicated to my husband, Jim. Your unwavering faith and belief in me are truly an inspiration. You are my best friend, lover, and lifetime companion. A man of few words, you are truly the wind beneath my wings. Thank you for supporting this first flight and for just being there with all the little crashes along the way to help put things back together. You bring balance and diversity to my life and make each day a new adventure.

"Hope, patience, and prayer will allow me to see opportunities instead of impossibilities."

# MRP AND BEYOND

## A Toolbox for Integrating People and Systems

CAROL A. PTAK, CFPIM, CIRM

**APICS**®

THE EDUCATIONAL SOCIETY FOR RESOURCE MANAGEMENT

**IRWIN**
*Professional Publishing*®
Chicago • London • Singapore

**Times Mirror**
**Higher Education Group**

**Library of Congress Cataloging-in-Publication Data**

Ptak, Carol A.
    MRP and beyond: a toolbox for integrating people and systems /
Carol A. Ptak.
        p. cm.
    ISBN 0-7863-0554-1
    Includes bibliographical references and index.
    1. Material requirements planning. 2. Production planning.
    I. Title.
    TS161.P79   1997
    658.5 20—dc20                                           96–33115

*Printed in the United States of America*
1 2 3 4 5 6 7 8 9 0 DOC 3 2 1 0 9 8 7 6

# C O N T E N T S

**Chapter 2**

## The Production Plan    21

**Chapter 3**

## Master Production Schedule (MPS)    41

**Chapter 6**

## Materials Requirements Planning (MRP)    105

**Chapter 9**

## Capacity Requirements Planning   157

**Chapter 10**

## The Right Tools for the Job   179

**Chapter 12**

# Beginning the Journey    215

# FOREWORD

Once in a great while, a teacher has the joy of encountering a student with immense potential and the energy and drive for great achievement. Anyone who has ever attended a presentation by the author, Carol Ptak, knows that she is one of these people. Carol approaches every task with zeal, commitment, and a focused mission in mind. Her mission in this book is to reach leaders and practitioners of small manufacturing firms with a vision—a vision of how computerized materials and capacity planning and control systems, now accessible on powerful microcomputers, can dramatically improve the daily operations of their businesses and serve as a key vehicle for executing a company's competitive strategies.

The book contains a wealth of insight obtained by implementing and utilizing several MRP systems over a period of nearly two decades in small manufacturing firms. Practitioners, especially, will appreciate the wisdom. It is the stuff of experience (and scar tissue) which, as Carol points out, is not taught in MRP school. It is the kind of knowledge that can keep one out of trouble and squeeze maximum leverage from the system.

From shop floor operator to plant operations manager to president of her own company, Carol has lived the life of the small manufacturer. It is no accident that this book begins with the subject of inventory, a large sinkhole for cash and a destroyer of competitive lead times. It also is no accident that the book closes on a strategic note. These are thoughtful opening and closing perspectives, crafted with an eye to owners and managers. Between these perspectives lie the information and wisdom that make it all work. Carol's view of various approaches to and facets of planning and control—MRP, JIT, theory of constraints, TQM, finite scheduling—is pragmatic. She points out that each of these serves particular purposes well. None of them is *the* answer. A business must draw from the available tools and approaches to craft a foundation for planning and control that is tailored to its own circumstances.

This is one of those intriguing books that "keeps on giving." No matter where you start, it will yield something of value. In the third or seventh reading, it will surprise you with an insight you didn't catch earlier because you weren't ready for it.

To the reader I say, this is a reference that should lead you to new depths of understanding and new heights of performance. To a former student who has learned to "fly with the eagles," I say, "Well done!"

**George Johnson, DBA, CFPIM**
**Professor of Operations Management and**
**Director of the APICS Industrial Inquiry Service**
**Rochester Institute of Technology**

# PREFACE

(6)

*MRP and Beyond* shows how MRP works and how this effective planning tool can fit into the development of a strategic excellence plan for the entrepreneurial business. The book enhances the basic idea of MRP, with a focus on process improvement. It is written in a readily understood form with many real-life examples from the small business context to illustrate key points. Computerized MRP dates to the early 1960s. Joseph Orlicky wrote the classic work on MRP in 1975. Due to the recent advent of affordable personal computer-based systems, materials requirements planning (MRP), capacity requirements planning (CRP), and manufacturing resource planning (MRP II) are some of the powerful planning tools now within the grasp of the small business. When these tools are integrated into an effective management toolbox, the entrepreneurial business can compete against companies many times its size.

Successful implementation of any integrated management system is dependent on some key actions. First, understanding your customers' needs and expectations is essential to establishing a meaningful planning system. Every company must have the same focus to stay in business—providing a quality product or service for a customer at a profit. Equally important is to understand the material flow process. Developing a meaningful planning system for a process that is not well understood is impossible. The breadth of individual responsibilities and the rapid growth of many entrepreneurial businesses make this understanding challenging yet achievable. In any successful company, the output of every process must fulfill the needs of the customer. The customer can be the next work area in the factory, the next process step in the service industry, or the final paying customer. Often the customer's highest priority is timely delivery of useable material. One method to accomplish this is by having large piles of inventory to buffer demand changes and process variability. Even though this may provide economies of scale, most entrepreneurial businesses cannot afford this significant investment in inventory. A better method is to control the process of material delivery and minimize variability. Optimizing the use of critical financial resources can mean the difference between success and bankruptcy for many entrepreneurial businesses.

## WHO SHOULD READ THIS BOOK

- **Entrepreneurial business owners.** Usually these are marketing or engineering personnel with little understanding of the field of material and production control.

- **Manufacturing personnel.** The company has grown too large to be controlled on the back of a 3 by 5 card. Working harder is not getting the job done. New tools are needed to effectively manage the company.

- **Production control and material control professionals new to the field.** Usually people in this field learn from others in the same field. However, in small companies there may be no one to learn from because there is no one else. This book communicates the results of years of experience, including mistakes and successes.

- **Frontline supervisors.** Any system implementation is extremely dependent on this group's understanding and support. This book clearly communicates why they are so important.

- **Inventory stock handlers, shipping and receiving personnel.** Transactions are needed to keep the system up to date. Accuracy is the responsibility of the process owner. Education of this group is a requirement for success.

- **Marketing management and sales personnel.** People from marketing and sales need to understand the full capability of the manufacturing side of the company. A high-performing manufacturing company harmonized with a closed-loop marketing and sales plan can be a strategic corporate weapon.

## HOW TO USE THIS BOOK

Entrepreneurial business professionals are constantly looking for a toolbox that is easily opened and used. *MRP and Beyond* provides many basic tools of manufacturing planning. Often, published works can only be understood with the assistance of a teacher, experienced professional, or consultant. *MRP and Beyond* does not need a translator. The author, an experienced small manufacturing professional, speaks the language of entrepreneurial business. In a typical entrepreneurial business, each person is responsible for many activities. The entrepreneurial spirit thrives, with everyone in the company going above and beyond the normal expectations of the job to service the customer. Time and other resources are in critical short supply. MRP enhances the productivity of these critical resources. Most books about integrated manufacturing planning systems are so complex that the business person feels overwhelmed and shies away from the ideas. From the perspective of the practitioner, *MRP and Beyond* describes basic steps and concepts in a step-by-step fashion that must be clearly understood to be successful.

*MRP and Beyond* begins with a look at the basic building block of manufacturing—inventory. Changes in manufacturing strategy have increased the amount of outside purchased material sharply. Understanding the inventory function and managing inventory effectively is essential for any company's success. The book then describes and applies the basic building blocks of MRP. The chapters can be used in sequence as a step-by-step approach for implementation or as a reference when encountering a challenge. Some material has been repeated in places to keep the reference helpful and complete without directing the reader to a different location. This book was designed to be used over and over. To quote George Johnson, Ph.D., CFPIM, "This is one of those intriguing books that 'keeps on giving.' No matter where you start, it will yield something of value. In the third or seventh reading, it will surprise you with an insight you didn't catch earlier because you weren't ready for it."

*MRP and Beyond* is written by an author who has been there and has learned by failure and success. These valuable lessons learned are blended into text examples. This book provides the tools for you to lay the cornerstone to a sturdy foundation for the future and to avoid pitfalls commonly encountered during the implementation.

# ACKNOWLEDGMENTS

I would first like to acknowledge the tireless work, dedication, and encouragement of William Latham, CFPIM, CIRM, without whose help this book would have remained a dream. He kept the manuscript on schedule and ensured that every "i" was dotted and "t" was crossed. I consider myself fortunate to be able to call Bill friend and colleague. Having a technical reviewer with much practical experience improved the caliber of this work.

I would also like to thank the entire staff at Intuitive Manufacturing Systems. All the system figures used in this book came from MRP9000™, a creative, leading edge MRP II system. We share the vision to bring this critical tool into the hands of every entrepreneurial business. Thank you for your continued support and encouragement.

Finally, I would like to acknowledge the technical and editorial review by George Johnson, Ph.D., CFPIM, from Rochester Institute of Technology (RIT). George has been my mentor for many years and was always there when I needed him.

# INTRODUCTION

Successful implementation of a material requirements planning system costs money. However, the benefits of a successful implementation exceed the costs. An effective MRP implementation will quickly return the initial financial investment and improve overall cash flow. Results used to justify the purchase and implementation costs include improved customer service, better on-time delivery, reduced inventory, higher productivity, revenue growth, and, best of all, improved profit. Since MRP reports by exception, instead of monitoring every part, planners and managers need respond only to exceptions and conditions outside the norm. This reduces expense for the manufacturing firm while improving operating results.

At the beginning of an implementation, a common philosophy and strategic direction must be developed concerning the future of the company and how it can successfully compete in its market. This vision must be communicated and understood throughout the firm. A common occurrence in small companies is that this vision stays in the mind of the entrepreneurial owner. Employees cannot help the company achieve its goals when they are not sure what the goals are. Without a vision, significant time is wasted developing controls and systems that do not move the business towards its strategic goal. After a vision has been established, the production plan and master production schedule can be used as continuing communication vehicles in the sales and operations planning process. The implementation helps define the structure that is required to support strategic objectives and operational plans. The structure includes plant layout, process definition (routings), and product definition (bills of material). Plant layouts and machinery groupings affect how units of capacity are defined. Only when this background work has been completed can choices like MRP and Capacity Requirements Planning (CRP) be successfully made. This may sound like a lot of work for an entrepreneurial business, but success can depend on it.

*MRP and Beyond* provides a basic understanding of these tools and how they can be applied to the process of managing a manufacturing business. The easy-to-read format and application examples provide a box of easily understood tools that can be selected to support a successful implementation. MRP is an excellent planning tool, providing forward visibility of component requirements for suppliers and planned availability of completed items for the customer. MRP is an essential building block for any closed-loop information system. It fits well with other tools such as Just-in-Time, Theory of Constraints, and Computer-Integrated Manufacturing. Gone are the days when entrepreneurial businesses only sell to other entrepreneurial businesses. Small companies have become suppliers for very large customers that may have sophisticated requirements for information technology. A successful MRP implementation is a sound foundation for the advanced quality systems required to compete in today's business environment.

Other options for visibility of material requirements are manual systems, including order point. These techniques were used successfully for many years. However, competitive pressures have changed the game. Increasing interest rates focused more companies on effectively managing inventory dollars. Cash flow is critical for most entrepreneurial businesses. This competitive business environment was ready for the development of automated techniques like MRP and CRP. MRP II closes the loop with finance to immediately recognize the financial impact of shop floor activities. This frees more valuable human resources to spend their time on exception conditions. Better planning prevents fire fighting and all the waste associated with it. Better planning means better visibility and better control. The rapidly decreasing cost of technology and computer software has finally put these sophisticated tools within the reach of every size company.

The future of manufacturing includes ever decreasing cycle times with ever increasing product options. Competition is fierce. Customers are quick learners. When current expectations are exceeded, expectations for the future rise. ISO 9000 requires control of the entire manufacturing process. Sixteen of the 17 requirements for ISO 9000 are fulfilled by a successful MRP II implementation. Accurate bills of material are essential for

Just-in-Time (JIT) pull techniques. Demand on a supplier's capacity can be scheduled into the future with the visibility of an MRP system. This is a strong foundation for developing supplier partnerships, because suppliers can plan rather than forecast their customers' demands and requirements. Since forecasts are always wrong and the techniques used to buffer errors costs money, integrating the demands of the company to the supplier can yield immediate positive results. Supplier partnerships have been proven to reduce cost of material. The cost of material averages 60 to 70 percent of the total cost of goods sold. Even a small reduction can have a big impact. Only when there is a strong foundation can a strong house be built using the best tools. A successful MRP implementation is a cornerstone of that foundation.

Successful implementation of these tools requires education about the control system requirements and expected results. Equally important, a thorough understanding of the overall business strategy and material process flow will result in the best application of the tools. A common understanding of this essential knowledge provides the means for successful communication among implementation team members and final users. This education must be provided for anyone involved with the management of inventory and capacity of the plant.

The material control process has its own language, foreign to people outside the field. Few current references address the unique needs of the entrepreneurial business with its critically short resources and multifunctional personnel. Most MRP implementations fail because education is neglected. Communication fails because there is not a common understanding of the language. People whom the system should benefit do not have a clear picture of what the results should look like. Similar to the lack of a communicated vision prohibiting maximum competitiveness, expecting people to change to a system they do not understand is unrealistic. Education is how a common language and vision is shared by all users of the system. Make your implementation go smoothly by involving everyone early in the process. Learn what questions to ask. *MRP and Beyond* gives you the basic building blocks to understand and successfully install an integrated planning system in an entrepreneurial business.

# 1

# ⑥ INVENTORY

## INTRODUCTION

To begin the exploration of material requirements planning, a basic understanding of inventory is required. Inventory is the lifeblood of every business. Manufacturing companies use inventory to build their final product. Distribution companies make a business of bringing in inventory in large quantities to be sent in smaller quantities to the final customers. Even service industries have inventory in the form of people who provide the services.

Understanding the importance of inventory to the overall success of the company requires an understanding of the different types and functions of inventory. On-hand inventory balances are the starting point for the Material Requirements Planning (MRP) calculations. Only when the beginning inventory record is accurate can MRP effectively provide accurate information to the users. Maintaining inventory record accuracy is a pivotal step in the overall effective management of the company. The human factor is extremely important to the accurate control of inventory. Any effective inventory control system must have a dedicated human element supporting it. The most sophisticated computer system is only as good as the people using it. Purchasing a world-class word processor does not make the purchaser the next Ernest Hemingway. Similarly, purchasing a world-class inventory control and planning system does not make a company a world-class producer.

To make a profit, a business takes inputs, performs a process to add value, and provides output to the customer at a price higher than the total cost of the inputs. Output may be physical products or it may be services. During the 1950s, managing inputs meant focusing on labor since it accounted for 50 to 60 percent of the cost of goods sold. The practice of spreading overhead by direct labor-hour came from the significance of the labor cost during that time. However, during the 1990s, the major factor in the cost of goods sold has shifted to material. The typical manufacturing company today has 60 to 75 percent of the cost of goods sold coming from material, as shown in Figure 1–1.

The increased percentage of material cost has justifiably intensified interest in the effective management of inventory, which can spell the difference between success and failure for a business. For example, look at the difference in a product with only a 10 percent improvement in the material cost:

|  | Before Improvement | After Improvement |
|---|---|---|
| Selling price: | $100.00 | $100.00 |
| Material cost: | $ 45.00 | $ 40.50 |
| Labor: | $ 7.50 | $ 7.50 |
| Overhead: | $ 22.50 | $ 22.50 |
| Total COGS: | $ 75.00 | $ 70.50 |
| Profit: | $ 25.00 | $ 29.50 |
| Profit increase: |  | + 18% |

The small 10 percent decrease in material cost ($4.50) yields an 18 percent increase in profits. What other activity can increase profits by this dramatic margin? When the possibility of decreasing inventory costs by 10 percent is balanced against the benefits, focusing on effective management of inventory is clearly an extremely effective way to directly improve the bottom line. The other beneficial operational impacts of a reduction of inventory further enhance bottom-line benefits. The ability to be nimble and responsive by having only what is required when it is required is an important competitive advantage.

F I G U R E   1–1

COGS Comparison

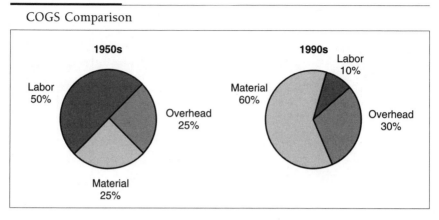

## INVENTORY TYPES

To effectively manage this valuable resource, the types and functions of inventory must be well understood. Commonly used classifications of inventory are raw materials, work in process (WIP), semifinished goods, finished goods, distribution inventories, and maintenance, repair, and operational supplies (MRO). The classification for a piece of inventory can change depending on its progress through the conversion process. In the simplified process flow diagram, raw materials are converted into work in process and then ultimately to finished goods to be sold to the customer.

### Raw Materials

These items are purchased by the company to be converted via the manufacturing process. A manufacturing company needs raw materials to build products for the customer. The value added by the manufacturer is really the product sold to the customer. Other names for this type of inventory are components, purchased details, or outside purchased (OP) parts. Examples of raw materials are empty circuit boards and electronic components. These are used by the circuit board assembler to make completed circuit boards. The empty circuit boards and electronic components are finished goods to their manufacturer but are raw materials to

**FIGURE 1–2**

Material Definition Evolution

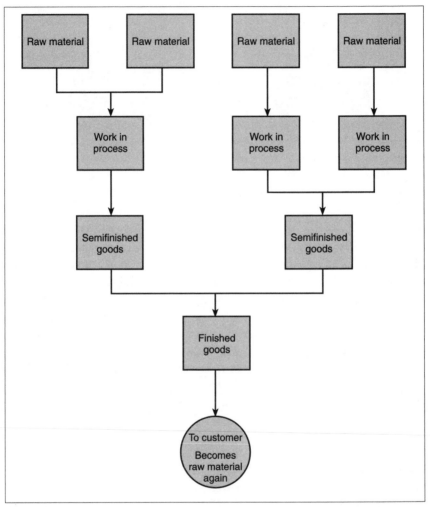

the circuit board assembler. Once assembled, these assembled circuit boards can then become raw materials to a computer manufacturer. The computer manufacturer takes these boards as raw materials and adds value by building them into a finished computer for shipment to the end customer, as shown in Figure 1–2. Except for industries where the raw materials are extracted from nature (mining, fishing, oil, etc.), all raw materials are purchased from outside the organization. In later chapters, different methods of ordering raw materials and determining the lot sizes will be discussed. Depending on the production environment and manufacturing strategy, different methods can be used to effectively manage this valuable resource. The biggest slice of the cost of goods sold currently comes from raw materials.

## Work in Process (WIP)

Some companies refer to this kind of inventory as work in progress or in-process inventory. All these terms mean exactly the same thing—raw materials that have started the value-adding activity in the plant. The raw materials have been moved from their storage location to a work area, and work has begun to change or assemble them into the finished product. This could be the electronic components on the shop floor in the automatic insertion equipment ready to be used to assemble boards. WIP is also the board waiting to be stuffed. Once the parts have been moved from their component inventory location, during the entire time these items are on the shop floor, the term *work in process* applies. Overhead costs may be applied to the material and/or the labor component. When lead times are very long, tracking work in process may be very important to the company. Just as taking a long trip requires more suitcases and materials than an overnight trip, long lead times mean there is a significant amount of inventory on the shop floor. Since the amount of work in process is large, the dollars associated with this inventory are also significant. Good financial management dictates tighter controls through detailed tracking. This is the main reason that manufacturing execution systems were developed.

The two factors determining the level of WIP inventory include lead time and order volume. Longer lead times require more WIP as material is staged through the production pipeline. Sufficient inventory must exist in the pipeline to ensure that critical capacity is not wasted due to shortage of materials. Costs that occur one month may go into a product that will be shipped several months down the road. Sophisticated tracking devices that keep track of work in process include bar coding, labor data collection systems, and daily time and attendance reports. As the order volume increases, the amount of WIP also increases given the same lead time. To move more water through a pipe, either the pipe gets bigger or the water moves faster. Similarly, WIP follows the same rules. When the rate increases, given the same lead time, the WIP increases proportionately. To keep the WIP at the same level during a rate increase, the lead time must decrease. WIP, lead time, and production rate are three adjustment knobs all tied to one another. Once the first two are determined, the third is also determined.

Shorter internal lead times have other beneficial effects. With shorter internal lead times, the controls on the work in process are simpler. Sophisticated tracking tools may not be required since the quantity and movement of inventory becomes very visible. The cost of implementing and operating these tracking tools is no longer exceeded by the benefit of increased visibility and control. Costs incurred one month are representative of product shipped during the same month. The cause and effect of a potential problem are close together in timing. Additional tracking and transactions to maintain history are no longer required. This reduction of lead time is a major focus for the "Just In Time" philosophy. Errors are easier to catch and correct when the level of work in process is low. The time from one process to the next is very small. When the time is small, the level of work in process is small. Although any disruption in the process will be felt immediately, the benefit is that any required rework will only affect a smaller quantity of parts. Tracking work in process can be critical to incorporate a change or process improvement. Most computer systems schedule the change of components and raw materials by date. Having low levels of work in process makes tracking to this expected date significantly easier since the subprocesses are more closely tied to the parent's schedule.

## Semifinished Goods

One way to shorten lead time to the final customer is to stock semifinished goods. These items have completed most of the value-added process but are waiting for a customer order. When the customer order arrives, semifinished goods can then be finished exactly to the customer's specifications. Some computer assemblers hold semifinished goods in modular form to be assembled into the configuration desired by the customer. The customer can order the computer with the desired specific configuration of hard drive, memory, floppy drives, monitor, and processing speed and still take delivery in a very short time. Waiting to assemble the finished product until the customer actually orders it reduces the risk of obsolete and unsalable inventory. This could be as simple as a final paint job or label or as complex as custom assembly, packaging, and distribution. Flexibility in responding to customer orders while minimizing inventory and the accompanying expense is a win-win situation. The customer gets a unique product in reduced time, and the manufacturer saves money and improves profits.

## Finished Goods

Finished goods are products sold to the customer. They have completed the entire conversion process in the plant. Other names for finished goods include finished product, end item, end product, and salable goods. External customers order finished goods from their suppliers. Remember that a finished good for one company can be a raw material for another. The overhead bins for an airplane are finished goods for the fabrication and assembly company but are raw materials for the airplane assembler. The material used to make the bin is raw material for the bin manufacturer but finished goods to the supplier.

Order quantities and the timing of orders for finished goods vary widely. This variation can come from many different factors, both internal and external to the customer. External factors can include the economy, competition, and the weather. For example, fresh cranberries are found only during the Thanksgiving holiday because the berries are extremely perishable and this is when the harvest takes place, not because of the holiday. Conversely, evergreen trees are in demand during December due to the holiday, not because they can be harvested only at this time. Many companies experience this type of external seasonality in the demand for finished goods such as snowmobiles, lawn mowers, boats, and golf clubs. External factors can also be manipulated by the news media and social norms. Recycled products have increased in demand due to aggressive marketing and changes in concerns about preserving the environment.

Internal factors are characteristics inherent to the product and the company. This includes pricing from the company, including specials, promotions, and sales. Retailers' January "white sales" promotion drives demand in the early part of the year for linens and sheets. This recurring increase in sales is due solely to the tradition of discount pricing during this time. The end-of-model year is an excellent time for buying a car to obtain a reduced price for last year's model. Many companies cause their own swings in market demand without realizing it through pricing and terms policies. Managing the market is not easy, but some companies have been successful in stabilizing demand. In the face of the traditional end-of-model year and end-of-month sales, Saturn, through its "no dicker" price policy, encourages customers to purchase cars throughout the year in a more level fashion. The level demand is easier for the company to fulfill through level production. The impact of level demand is felt through the entire supply chain.

The effect of variability of demand for finished goods is felt at the supplier level for component materials. Since the customer does not want to hold the inventory, the supplier is expected to deliver the product just before it is needed. Many different techniques are used in an attempt to have finished goods available when the customer expects them. One alternative is to vary production capacity to meet the demands of the customer. The opposite choice is to keep capacity constant and vary the amount of inventory. Mixing and blending these two techniques to best support the customer is also an option. Managing and implementing these techniques will be explained in later chapters.

## Distribution Inventory

Many companies do not ship directly to the final customer but use a distribution system. This system includes shipping in bulk to consolidated warehouses or distribution points. The warehouses or distribution points then ship the smaller quantities to the end user. The purpose behind this is to save money and better service the customer. The goal of using a distribution network should be lower total transportation costs because it is cheaper to ship full truckloads long distances and then break the large lots down to provide smaller lots to the customer over shorter distances. Grocery stores have mastered this process with amazing efficiency. Individual stores are restocked nightly based on sales during the day. Due to the efficiency of the distribution system, the large stocks in the grocery store back room have disappeared. The result is lower spoilage, less waste, and improved customer service. Managing the level of inventory in the system is extremely challenging. Sufficient inventory is required to fulfill customers' demands without wasting precious resources on unwanted inventory. The art of distribution management encompasses the activities of transportation, inventory control, material handling, warehousing, order administration, packaging, and communication systems.

## Maintenance, Repair, and Operational Supplies (MRO)

MRO items support the manufacturing operations without being part of the finished product shipped to the customer. For example, they include grease and oil for machines, gloves, tape, shop coats, drill bits, and so on. Controlling the inventory of these items is especially challenging because the usage levels for some items stay constant no matter what the production volume while others increase as the production volume increases. MRO items usually receive little attention until a shortage causes the manufacturing process to stop. The common reaction is to stock a large quantity to ensure that parts are always available. Even though this means that each part is less expensive since it was purchased in bulk, large stockpiles can require a large financial investment. The money invested in carrying large inventories can be utilized better elsewhere. The alternative is to develop supplier partnerships, restocking programs, and blanket purchase orders for these items. These approaches can yield a positive impact to material availability and cost. This is another case of a win-win situation when inventory is effectively managed. The customer (manufacturer) is better served at a lower cost to the company, therefore increasing profits.

## INVENTORY FUNCTIONS

The different types of inventory—raw materials, work in process, semifinished goods, finished goods, and distribution inventory—can serve different functions: anticipation, fluctuation, lot size, transportation, and/or hedge. These functions are not limited by the type of inventory. Understanding the underlying function of inventory is essential to developing appropriate control measures for this critical investment.

### Anticipation

Anticipation inventory is increased when supplies are expected to decrease or demand is expected to increase suddenly. This could result from normally expected seasonal variation, such as lawn mowers selling better in the spring, or supply problems due to winter storms or labor strikes. A management decision must be made to adjust the inventory levels to respond to expected changes. One alternative is to have manufacturing build to a steady rate all year. The excess is stockpiled from the off-season to provide required inventory for the busy season. This manufacturing philosophy is the least disruptive to manufacturing but usually is the highest inventory level alternative. The cost of running out of inventory and/or the cost of disruption to manufacturing is compared to the cost of carrying inventory to determine if inventory is the best alternative. Even if the cost is beneficial to carry inventory, if the product is perishable, this solution is not feasible. In this case, surge capacity to match the needs of the market is required. Another possibility is to utilize stable semifinished goods that can be completed ahead of time for assembly at the last possible moment.

### Fluctuation

One of the ways to guard against shortage due to unexpected variation in usage is to increase inventory levels. This variation can come from unreliable quality of the raw material or conversion process, forecast error, unreliable lead times, or anything else that causes an unexpected change in supply or demand.

Fluctuation inventory is most commonly known as safety stock. The level of safety stock can be calculated to provide desired customer service levels when the amount of previous variation is known. This technique is further explored in the forecasting section of Chapter 3.

Safety stock is most commonly held at the level immediately before or after the cause of the variability. Safety stocks of raw materials are used to guard against suppliers not delivering on time or having questionable quality. Safety stocks of raw material can also be used to guard against variability of demand for finished goods if the conversion process can be accomplished quickly. If the conversion process through work in process is long, the decision may be made to use finished goods as fluctuation inventory. An example is the clothing industry. When the total lead times are considered for the acquisition of cloth and the conversion into clothing, the amount of finished goods is predetermined and stocked. The highest cost fluctuation inventory is finished goods and distribution inventory. All the labor and material have been added to these items. If the item does not sell and the product is obsolete, the capacity to build the item can never be recovered. In a rapidly growing company, this capacity could have been used to build something else that would have been sold at a profit. Considering the costs to carry and to discard this inventory and the opportunity cost of the resources used, using finished goods as fluctuation inventory can be a triple loss. The level of fluctuation inventory should be a careful business decision of investment and return.

## Lot Size

The amount of inventory ordered at a time is called lot size or order quantity. Lot size inventory results from price breaks from suppliers, packaging conventions, setup costs, shipping costs, or characteristics of the manufacturing process. Eggs are a great example of packaging conventions causing lot size inventory. Hens produce the product one at a time, but the long-standing tradition has been to package them in lot sizes of a dozen. Consumer demand for other lot sizes has caused packages of 6 and

18 to appear on the shelf. The eggs left over after the recipe has been completed are lot size inventory.

In manufacturing, dies or any equipment requiring significant setup causes lot size inventory. Generally there is a trade-off between the quantity produced and the time required to set up the equipment. The longer the machine takes to set up, the larger the run. This is calculated using a technique called economic order quantity (EOQ). The EOQ relates the cost of the item, anticipated demand, inventory carrying cost, and setup cost to calculate the optimal order size. Using an economic order quantity always results in carrying an amount of lot size inventory.

The economic order quantity, although very old, is still used to determine the order of magnitude of the optimal order size. Many people get carried away using the EOQ formula and attempt to apply it inappropriately. The resulting appearance of mathematical precision has led some people to order in exact EOQ quantities like 139 even though there was a significant discount at a 150 order quantity. The sensitivity of the formula must be considered when making the final lot size decision. Overall cost, customer service issues, and production efficiency also play a part.

EOQ still has a fit in the process that experiences long setup times and comparatively shorter run times. The business environment must need all the parts calculated by the EOQ. If the company has only make-to-order demand and the EOQ calculates a lot quantity higher than the demand, the extra parts should not be made just for the sake of EOQ. EOQ is an approximation of the order quantity. The calculation gives the appearance of precision, but the resulting order quantity is really just a guideline.

The EOQ formula is $\sqrt{\dfrac{2US}{IC}}$ , where:

U  =  annual expected usage in units.
S  =  setup cost in dollars.
I  =  inventory carrying cost expressed as an annual percentage.
C  =  the cost of the item in dollars.

The resulting order quantity will be in units of production.

**U:** The annual expected usage in units can be either the historic consumption of the past year or the forecast usage based on the master schedule for the upcoming year.

**S:** The setup cost in dollars includes all the costs associated with changing from one production run to another. Setup time can be considered as the time from the last good part of the previous run to the first good part of the next run. All costs associated with that time and procedure should be included in the setup costs. Usually these times are estimated in terms of hours of production and are costed by applying a standard labor rate for the area and adding overhead burden. For purchased parts these costs include the entire order preparation cost for the purchasing department. The costs are added for each purchase order as it moves through the receipt process, receiving inspection, storage, and invoice payment. The traditional approach is to add all overhead costs and divide by the number of purchase orders issued during that time period. The caution is that some purchase orders take significantly more time than others. For the purposes of calculating the economic order quantity, the average is sufficient.

**I:** The inventory carrying cost is one of the most difficult costs to determine. The most frequent way this cost is determined is by asking the head of the finance department. This person usually has some strong feelings concerning the value of the money currently tied up in inventory. A rough estimation can be made by adding the cost of borrowing money to the cost of running the warehouse, including the people, computer systems, and floor space. Other factors to be included in the cost of carrying inventory are the risk of obsolescence, damage, theft, or spoilage. After all the quantitative factors are considered, the norm for inventory carrying costs is in the range of 40 to 70 percent per year.

**C:** The cost of the item used in the EOQ formula is usually the fully loaded cost, including overhead, used to value the inventory for bookkeeping purposes. These costs include material, labor, overhead, and outplant services.

**Example:**

| | |
|---|---|
| Annual usage: | 3500 parts |
| Carrying cost: | 40% |
| Item cost: | $137.25 |
| Setup cost: | 6 hours at a fully loaded shop rate of $20/hr. |

EOQ: $$\sqrt{\frac{2 \times 3500 \times \$120}{.40 \times \$137.25}} = 124 \text{ units}$$

Other lot size techniques that order more than the immediate needs result in residual lot size inventory. The most common cause for lot size inventory is purchasing discounts and the trade-off between setup costs and inventory costs.

## Transportation

This inventory is also known as pipeline inventory. Parts coming from suppliers require lead time to arrive at the customer's place of business. This time can be very short if the supplier is local or the transportation method is rapid, like air freight. Similar to work in process, with a short lead time the inventory in the pipeline should be very little. As the transportation time increases, inventory in the pipeline increases proportionately. Transportation inventory can be significant if the supplier is a long distance away or the transportation method is slow, like water carriers. Even though the cost of an individual part may be lower from a supplier that is further away, the cost of transportation itself and carrying the transportation inventory make the true cost higher. With increasing costs of carrying inventory, local suppliers are favored because of favorable transportation inventory costs and improved response agility.

## Hedge

Sometimes raw material cost or availability is affected by the world commodity markets or political pressures. There can be a shortage on the supply of a semiconductor, and supply of that component may be put on an allocation basis. Orders are not filled completely but at a smaller percentage of the requested amount. When drastic changes in market prices are expected, the purchaser may choose to carry extra inventory as insurance. This extra inventory is called hedge inventory. Similar to fluctuation inventory, hedge inventory is most commonly held at the raw material level. Stocking hedge inventory can be very expensive and risky. The company can be placed in the position of holding inventory when the market price declines. Using hedge inventory can be compared to playing the stock market. Sometimes you win; sometimes you lose. You have little control over the rules of the game or the market. If you are smart (or lucky) in the long run, the risk and return balance each other.

## MANAGING INVENTORY

Successful inventory management is a challenging part of managing the overall business. Determining the correct level of inventory is something like the fable of the three bears. On one side, too little inventory usually provides poor customer service and manufacturing inefficiency. The adage is that you cannot sell from an empty wagon. On the other hand, too much inventory also can provide poor customer service and manufacturing inefficiency. When too much inventory is on hand, the business has a difficult time reacting to changes in the market. Too much inventory on the shop floor causes confusion and wasted effort. Orders go to the competitor who can respond most effectively to the customer's expectation. The "just right" level of inventory provides excellent customer service and allows the business to enjoy a profitable existence and continued growth.

Effective management of the functions and purposes of inventory requires understanding the role inventory must play in the production process and the strategic position in the marketplace. In a company's financial reporting, inventory is carried on the balance sheet as an asset. The value of the inventory is usually second only to capital assets such as equipment and plants. Ensuring record accuracy and safekeeping, this asset is a "people" issue, not a computer issue. People make the system; people can break the system. Understanding how the system and company financial results are affected by various actions is key to a company's success. A key tool in effectively managing inventory is maintaining high record accuracy.

## Maintaining Inventory Record Accuracy

There is an industry in which every piece of inventory is accounted for and balanced every night before anyone goes home. Unheard of? Too expensive? The industry is banking. Its inventory is money, both figuratively and literally. At its basic function, the bank is a stockroom, tracking receipts and issues. At the end of each day, the store's records are balanced. Clearly the expectation is that its inventory record accuracy must be 100 percent.

Banks have the advantage of interchangeable inventory. An accurate balance can be maintained even if there are more five's than expected if there is a balancing reduction in other denominations. Manufacturing companies are not that fortunate. Steel cannot be substituted for semiconductors. Accuracy must be maintained for every item. This requirement does not change just because the inventory process is automated. Accuracy is important for any system to be useful, whether it is manual or automatic. For any MRP system to provide worthwhile information, inventory record accuracy is critical. This will be further explored in subsequent chapters. When the tool is expanded to include MRP II, inventory accuracy has a direct impact on the financial condition of the company. When a quantity of parts is reported as lost, an automatic general ledger transaction is created that decreases the amount of inventory asset. Since the balance sheet must stay in balance, the corresponding decrease is also seen in the owner's equity.

How can inventory accuracy be established and maintained? The answer is discipline. Discipline is not easy. Well-disciplined stockrooms do not need chainlink-locked fences, barbed wire, or limited access. Simple systems can be established that everyone understands, appreciates, and uses. These systematic process controls yield exceptionally high inventory accuracy. Just as inspection cannot be used to improve quality, padlocks and chainlink fences cannot be used to improve accuracy. Some of the most inaccurate storage areas are those behind locked doors.

The key to discipline is ownership. Every person cares for what she owns. When inventory is viewed as the property of another function or department, accuracy is unachievable. The people responsible for the inventory must also be accountable. Getting inventory out of storage areas by circumventing the system becomes an exciting challenge for many manufacturing personnel. Their creativity and cunning are remarkable. The overall mission of production personnel is to add value to component inventory for shipment to a customer. Making access to component inventory difficult seems contrary to the mission, but many companies do just that. There is a fence with guards between the production people and their inventory. The highest inventory record accuracy occurs when the ownership and accountability belong to the users of the inventory. Assign inventory to the production workforce, including the counting and validating of inventory record accuracy. People learn quickly that a part removed without recording that activity leads to part shortages and frustration further down the road. This is consistent with the overall process improvement approach where the process is owned by the person who has the most to gain or lose from the output.

## Physical Inventory

Two of the most common ways to monitor inventory record accuracy are physical inventory and cycle counting. Physical inventory occurs when all activity in the shop stops and everyone in the company goes to the stockroom to count parts. From the perspective of the people involved, the primary objective of this activity is to be done as quickly as possible, without regard for the impact of incorrect counts and mishandling of parts. They do not have to live with the results. The aftermath of an annual physical inventory can take months to remedy. During one annual physical inventory, a person unfamiliar with the parts was found counting integrated circuit chips (ICs) by stripping them out of their static protected sheaths and placing them on a scale to bulk weigh them. Since ICs are extremely sensitive to static discharge, this activity cost the company many thousands of dollars to replace damaged parts and disrupted the shop due to part shortages. The company decided never to do another physical inventory. There had to be a better way. The alternative to a physical inventory is cycle counting.

## Cycle Counting

Cycle counting is an ongoing process check on the accuracy of inventory transactions. To start cycle counting, a control group of parts is selected. This is a small number of parts that can be counted on a daily basis in less than one hour. The group should contain parts that are expensive and inexpensive, rapidly moving and slow moving, big and small. The control group is counted daily and compared to the inventory record. If there is any discrepancy between the actual count and the record amount, an investigation is completed to determine the cause. Any required adjustment to the on-hand count is done after the investigation. More importantly, the inventory control process is improved to eliminate the cause. Only after 10 consecutive days of 100 percent accuracy in the control group with no adjustments or investigation should the counts on other parts begin. This is the step that most companies skip in the hurry to correct on-hand counts. The control group step is the most important because it is an excellent way to identify and correct process issues. When process issues have been corrected for the control group, they are corrected for the balance of the inventory. The overall inventory accuracy can rise more quickly and be maintained at a higher level more easily.

Once the control group has maintained its accuracy for 10 days, the counting exercise can be expanded to the balance of the inventory. In cycle counting, every day some parts are selected and counted. These counts are compared against the perpetual inventory record. Any errors are investigated and corrected. The items selected for daily counts can be chosen from a number of different ways. The most common methods are:

- **Calendar frequency using ABC classification.** A decision is made on how frequently to cycle through the parts. This is the classic cycle count procedure.
- **Order time.** At the time the part is ordered, inventory should be low. Validating inventory at this time can prevent overordering parts.
- **Receipt time.** By this time the inventory should be at its absolute lowest. Completing the count should be quick and easy.
- **Negative inventory.** This is a clear indication that the inventory control process is out of control. Usually a receipt transaction was not done or a work order was issued twice. Negative inventory should be rectified on a daily basis.
- **Inventory location.** This approach can identify previously misplaced parts. Instead of counting by item number, everything in an inventory location is counted. Judgment is used to count only those parts that are easy to count or with an obvious error. Using valuable time to track and resolve items only with a problem will yield better benefits, including the ability to count more parts.

Chapter 5 discusses in more detail how to develop and implement an effective cycle counting program, including a how to–step-by-step approach.

## SUMMARY

An effective inventory process is an essential part of every successful company. Inventory is the lifeblood of every service and manufacturing company. Controlling inventory and knowing how much inventory exists can make the difference between a business's success and failure. A business that does not know how much inventory it has can waste scarce resources by purchasing material or services it will not use. Even worse is not having the correct material on hand to deliver products to the customer.

Inventory goes through many stages during its progression to the final customer. Beginning as raw material, it becomes work in process when work begins on it. After completing its process in the manufacturing plant, inventory becomes finished goods, ready to ship to the customer. Again, inventory changes identity and becomes raw material, work in process, and, finally, finished goods. This process occurs over and over until the inventory moves into distribution for delivery to the end customer.

Businesses can fail when the process of managing inventory is not well understood and managed. Small businesses have a critical need for cash. Inventory sitting on the shelf ties up cash and does not pay the bills. Managing inventory well can be a key tool for success. A very important part of managing inventory is knowing how much of the different types and functions of inventory is in the plant. Challenging the underlying reasons for having inventory can dramatically reduce the need for inventory. Inventory levels are a result of other business processes. More variability results in higher inventory. As these underlying processes are improved, the level of inventory should decrease.

On-hand inventory balances are the starting point for Material Requirements Planning (MRP) calculations. Only when the beginning inventory record is accurate can MRP effectively provide accurate information to the users. Maintaining inventory record accuracy is a pivotal step in the overall effective management of the company. High levels of inventory record accuracy require discipline and commitment. The investment in record accuracy is worthwhile when compared to the chaos caused by inaccurate inventory. Like all things in life, the important ones are rarely easy. Effectively managing inventory is no exception.

# 2

# THE PRODUCTION PLAN

## INTRODUCTION

The production plan is one of the most useful and most over-looked tools for managing manufacturing. The goals and objectives of a manufacturing company are communicated to manufacturing via the production plan. This plan balances the strategic goals of the company with the available capacity. The production plan includes planned increases or decreases in inventory and/or production rates. The overall level of manufacturing output is defined in the plan. Once the level of manufacturing output is known, budgets, resource planning, and cash flow projections can be computed. The concise plan for manufacturing output defines how the customer will be served, the inventory strategy, and the resulting financial impact for the company. Since the production plan is usually stated in dollars (the universal language) for each product family, the process of establishing the plan is a communication opportunity for all functional areas. Once the plan is established and the focus moves to tactical execution through the master production schedule and MRP, each functional area focuses on its own unique language and issues. Development of the production plan is a strategic, cross-functional team activity for senior management. The development process allows everyone to be involved and committed to the resulting plan.

The production plan is the coarse adjustment knob for the business. The production planning process is a critical tool in the business toolbox of any size company.

A goal of shipping $5 million in product in one week is great, but if the company's total sales for the entire previous year were $3 million, it is unlikely the goal will be met. A realistic balance is required between goals and critical resource capacities. Too often a small company thinks that the planning process is not required due to its size, and the plan is kept solely in the mind of the founder or president. Only when the production plan is communicated to other people in the company can they help fulfill the vision. In the face of an unknown production plan, investments are made dependent on the "project of the day" rather than on an overall long-term company plan. Using a production plan gets the direction for the company out of one person's head into others' hands so the company can grow, develop, and achieve its full potential.

## THE PRODUCTION-PLANNING PROCESS

When the production-planning process is used, better decisions can be made for investing the company's critical resources because there is a better understanding of the needs and consequences of the decisions. Many interesting business opportunities exist, especially for the entrepreneurial company. Some items and investments cannot be accomplished because something else was more critical to the overall success of the business. Priority must be placed on more critical activities and investments. Once the company begins using the production-planning process, the business moves to a long-term view and long-term success. The production plan is the long-term planning tool for any size company in any industry. Remember, "We never plan to fail, we only fail to plan."

The real value of the production plan is not the time-phased schedule of product families but the identification of the resource constraints to making the plan a reality. This can be compared to playing on a teeter-totter. This child's toy clearly shows how an imbalance between two loads can stop the whole game. Consider that the production plan is on one side of the teeter-totter and resources are on the other. Just as having someone 40 pounds heavier than you on the other side leaves you dangling your feet in the breeze going nowhere fast, having a major imbalance between the production plan and capacity has the same impact on the company. It goes nowhere fast, and everyone involved feels frustrated.

Identifying constraints to output is a key requirement for developing a realistic production plan. Constraints are items that limit the output of the company. For example, the critical constraint for small businesses is cash. Many times a small company is presented with a great idea or market to capitalize on but cannot pursue it due to financial constraints. The production plan can help identify future resource issues that would prevent fulfillment of the strategic plan before these issues become a crisis. Large companies can benefit from diversified products and business units that can be used to fund start-ups and new product development. The small business has to make each dollar count just to ensure its existence.

The development of a high-quality production plan involves many people and management issues. Good team skills are required to ensure that everyone gets a say; however, it is usually impossible for everyone to get their way. In the absence of an integrated production plan, marketing has its plan, which is second-guessed by production control. In turn, manufacturing second-guesses the plan from production control. Unless the company is small enough where all functions are performed by the same person, second-guessing can have everyone pulling in different directions. Each function or person will attempt to do

**FIGURE  2–1**

Integrated Production Planning Process

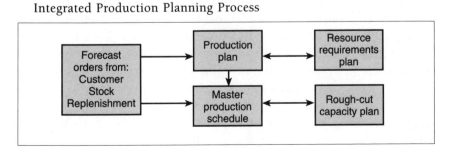

what she thinks is best for her area. The lack of unity decreases the effectiveness of the entire organization.

Small business is agile and can change quickly. In small companies, rapid changes are sometimes not communicated to other areas of the same organization until after a problem develops in that area. This quick reactivity is a perfect example of how a strength for the business can also become a weakness. As a result, the overall organization is not well served, nor is the customer. The production plan can help communicate the changes in strategy to all affected parties in the company.

Every manufacturing company, no matter what size, takes inputs, does something to them, and delivers them to a customer as output. This conversion process accumulates costs during the acquisition of the components and during the conversion itself. To remain in business, a company must sell the results of the process to a customer at a price higher than the company's total costs. If the customer does not like what is being sold or the completed product does not have value sufficient for the price, the customer will buy elsewhere. This is the basis of a free market economy. Even if the customer is not the stated direct focus for the company, the power of supply and demand drives the focus eventually to the customer. The production plan is the way to communicate that focus. On a more detailed basis, the master production schedule provides visibility, at a part number level, of the expected build schedule. This integrated planning process then plans all the materials, capacity, and other resources to be available so that what the customer wants can be delivered when it is desired.

The actual master production schedule at the end-item level is entirely different from the production plan in the same way a penny is different from a dollar. The penny is a smaller unit of measure of money, just as the master production schedule is a smaller unit of measure of the production plan. Pennies can be added up and spent like dollar bills, but no matter how hard you try, you cannot take 100 pennies and turn them into paper money without going to the bank. Similarly, the master production schedule further defines and details the production plan. When added together, the master schedule bears a resemblance to the production plan but is not identical to the production plan without a significant unit of measure conversion. Different resource types are used to validate each plan.

## Forecasting and the Production Plan

The first step in developing a production plan is to forecast sales. The production plan is not necessarily the sales plan. Sales can be irregular and seasonal. The company may choose to produce in a level method and allow inventory to build in anticipation of the busy season. The other choice is to have flexible capacity and build in match step with sales. The choice of method is dependent on the relative cost of each and the feasibility of the capacity requirements. The initial product family sales forecasts communicate the need for products. The production plan communicates the production strategy and the requirements for resources.

Forecasting inherently has some drawbacks. There are three basic rules of forecasting.

**1. Forecasts are always wrong.** No matter how hard you try, it is virtually impossible to hit the forecast right on the nose. When the forecast is exactly right, it is like hitting the lottery. However, the forecasting process and the forecast itself still have value. The forecast is the best available estimate of future sales. This allows long lead time materials to be placed on order and long lead time resources to be acquired.

**2. Forecasts are less accurate farther into the future.** The second rule of using forecasts is that the farther into the future the forecast goes, the larger the degree of error. Forecasting the near future is always more accurate since it bears the closest resemblance to the current state.

**3. Forecasts are less accurate when finer detail is used.** The last rule of forecasting is that forecasts are always more accurate in larger time buckets. To illustrate, think of how much money you have in your pocket right now. That is like forecasting today's business. The level of accuracy should be fairly high. Now forecast how much money you will have in your pocket six years from today. This is virtually impossible to guess! Next, attempt to forecast how much money you have today, but now instead of just total dollars, you want to know in specific denominations—pennies, nickels, dimes, quarters, dollars, fives, tens, and so on. Which is more accurate, the detailed forecast or the accumulated forecast? Of course the accumulated forecast is more accurate. When attempting to forecast how much money you will have in your pocket six years from now in that fine level of denomination detail, your chance of being accurate is significantly less than winning the lottery or being struck by lightning. The same effect is seen in attempting to forecast a business's activities far into the future in fine detail.

Breaking down the production plan into small time buckets closer to the current period trades the accuracy of the closer period with the inaccuracy of the smaller time bucket. As future plans are made, larger time buckets are used for aggregate planning. The production plan for three years into the future is likely in annual numbers. The production plan for next month has most likely been further refined into weekly targets. The most important thing about the production plan is that the breakdown should be done such that the plan is fit for use by the next step in the planning process. The sales forecast in turn drives the production plan. The starting place for the acquisition of resources is this top-level production plan. The production plan is a long-term strategic plan. Therefore, the resources planned by the production plan are long lead resources like new plant buildings, critical machines, and overall headcount. Many different people use this plan and desire to have it represented differently.

## Representing the Production Plan

The production plan can be expressed in a table format as shown in Table 2–1 or in a graphical format as shown in Figure 2–2. The choice of display format is purely one of personal preference. Graphs make relative volume comparisons easier, while tables are needed for accurate calculations. Time is accumulated into different size periods called time buckets. Notice that in Table 2–1, the time buckets are different sizes depending on the horizon: the closer to current, the smaller the bucket; the farther out, the larger the bucket. This is done for two reasons. First, in the near future, smaller pieces of the plan are easier to manage more effectively. The plan is translated into more detailed daily and

**TABLE 2-1**

KC Manufacturing Production Plan

| Product Groups | Jan | Feb | Mar | Apr | May | June | 3rd Q | 4th Q | 1st Q | 2nd Q | Next Year | Year After |
|---|---|---|---|---|---|---|---|---|---|---|---|---|
| | | | | | | *Production Plan ($ in thousands)* | | | | | | |
| RGB customer | 12 | 13 | 15 | 15 | 15 | 15 | 40 | 50 | 55 | 60 | 180 | 195 |
| ERT customer | 20 | 10 | 20 | 10 | 20 | 25 | 60 | 75 | 75 | 60 | 200 | 350 |
| QWR customer | 15 | 13 | 13 | 15 | 15 | 15 | 50 | 60 | 60 | 75 | 250 | 350 |
| Others | 20 | 20 | 20 | 20 | 20 | 20 | 60 | 60 | 60 | 70 | 280 | 350 |
| OEM Total | $67 | $56 | $68 | $60 | $70 | $75 | $210 | $245 | $250 | $265 | $910 | $1,245 |
| Commercial | 25 | 35 | 40 | 50 | 25 | 50 | 100 | 110 | 80 | 60 | 450 | 550 |
| Prototypes | 10 | 12 | 12 | 15 | 12 | 13 | 35 | 35 | 35 | 35 | 150 | 150 |
| Total | $102 | $103 | $120 | $125 | $107 | $138 | $345 | $390 | $365 | $360 | $1,510 | $1,945 |

weekly plans for execution. Weekly and daily plans have little significance one to two years into the future.

The same data were used and the production plan was normalized by dividing by the number of months involved so that the impact of the projected growth rate can be clearly seen.

In either format, the real power of this information is to determine the overall resources required to run the business. These resources can be material, supplier capacity, skilled labor availability, facilities, or cash. At KC Manufacturing the management team has determined that the critical resources are cash investment, plant square footage, and computer numerically controlled (CNC) machine capacity. These resources are the items that limit the amount of output. The company has tracked the need for these resources based on historical output rates. Ratios of resources to output are then used to bring real meaning to the impact of the production plan. Table 2–2 identifies the need for these critical resources for each $1,000 in production plan dollars.

As would be expected, the level of investment needed for custom prototype work exceeds the higher-rate production for the OEM customers. The plant square footage and machine hours are also increased due to the custom nature of this work. With

F I G U R E   2–2

Production Plan Revenue $/Month

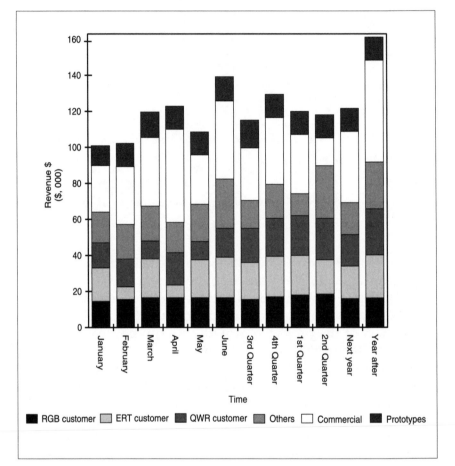

this intensity of resources, the profit margin is also expected to be higher. Otherwise, the company would logically avoid prototype work. One reason to still take prototype work without higher margins is that the prototype work is how the company develops new products for future markets. This can be considered a long-term investment in the company's growth and future. The translation of the production plan to required resources clearly demonstrates to the management team the commitment required to achieve production goals.

**T A B L E   2–2**

Resource Requirements

| Project Groups | Cash Required (in thousands) | Plant Square Footage | CNC Machine Hours |
|---|---|---|---|
| RGB customer | $  250 | 250 | 5 |
| ERT customer | 250 | 250 | 5 |
| QWR customer | 250 | 250 | 5 |
| Others | 250 | 250 | 5 |
| *OEM Total* | $1,000 | 1,000 | 20 |
| *Commercial* | 300 | 200 | 7 |
| *Prototypes* | 400 | 300 | 10 |

Calculating the critical resources from the production plan brings information to light that may have gone unnoticed during the routine running of the business. Small businesses must spend each unit of critical resource wisely to ensure future survival. The production plan and resulting resource plan allow the management team to view these requirements in a strategic way. The resource plans for each of the critical resources are summarized in a table format in Table 2–3.

In this example, the need for cash generation stays fairly level with some increase noted in the year after next year as demonstrated in Table 2–4. This cash budget is extremely valuable to the financial planning of the business. For the company to remain viable, the sources of cash must exceed the need for this critical resource.

Obviously plant square footage cannot be added or subtracted in small pieces. In addition, the plant square footage remains after each month's production is completed. For these reasons the data were normalized back to the square footage required by month. Provided that KC Manufacturing has at least a 33,000-square-foot manufacturing facility, projected business volumes should fit into the current facility. Given the rate of growth, however, the management team can determine from these data the early warning that additional space may be required by year three. Either additional space must be secured by year three or a

# TABLE 2-3

KC Manufacturing Resource Plan

**Cash Required**

| Product Groups | Jan | Feb | Mar | Apr | May | June | 3rd Q | 4th Q | 1st Q | 2nd Q | Next Year | Year After |
|---|---|---|---|---|---|---|---|---|---|---|---|---|
| RGB customer | 3,000 | 3,250 | 3,750 | 3,750 | 3,750 | 3,750 | 10,000 | 12,500 | 13,750 | 15,000 | 45,000 | 48,750 |
| ERT customer | 5,000 | 2,500 | 5,000 | 2,500 | 5,000 | 6,250 | 15,000 | 18,750 | 18,750 | 15,000 | 50,000 | 87,500 |
| QWR customer | 3,750 | 3,250 | 3,250 | 3,750 | 3,750 | 3,750 | 12,500 | 15,000 | 15,000 | 18,750 | 62,500 | 87,500 |
| Others | 5,000 | 5,000 | 5,000 | 5,000 | 5,000 | 5,000 | 15,000 | 15,000 | 15,000 | 17,500 | 70,000 | 87,500 |
| *OEM Total* | $16,750 | $14,000 | $17,000 | $15,000 | $17,500 | $18,750 | $52,500 | $61,250 | $62,500 | $66,250 | $227,500 | $311,250 |
| *Commercial* | 7,500 | 10,500 | 12,000 | 15,000 | 7,500 | 15,000 | 30,000 | 33,000 | 24,000 | 18,000 | 135,000 | 165,000 |
| *Prototypes* | 4,000 | 4,800 | 4,800 | 6,000 | 4,800 | 5,200 | 14,000 | 14,000 | 14,000 | 14,000 | 60,000 | 60,000 |
| Total | $28,250 | $29,300 | $33,800 | $36,000 | $29,800 | $38,950 | $96,500 | $108,250 | $100,500 | $98,250 | $422,500 | $536,250 |

# TABLE 2-4

KC Manufacturing Resource Plan

**Cash Required**

| Product Groups | Jan | Feb | Mar | Apr | May | June | 3rd Q | 4th Q | 1st Q | 2nd Q | Next Year | Year After |
|---|---|---|---|---|---|---|---|---|---|---|---|---|
| RGB customer | 3,000 | 3,250 | 3,750 | 3,750 | 3,750 | 3,750 | 10,000 | 12,500 | 13,750 | 15,000 | 45,000 | 48,750 |
| ERT customer | 5,000 | 2,500 | 5,000 | 2,500 | 5,000 | 6,250 | 15,000 | 18,750 | 18,750 | 15,000 | 50,000 | 87,500 |
| QWR customer | 3,750 | 3,250 | 3,250 | 3,750 | 3,750 | 3,750 | 12,500 | 15,000 | 15,000 | 18,750 | 62,500 | 87,500 |
| Others | 5,000 | 5,000 | 5,000 | 5,000 | 5,000 | 5,000 | 15,000 | 15,000 | 15,000 | 17,500 | 70,000 | 87,500 |
| *OEM Total* | 16,750 | 14,000 | 17,000 | 15,000 | 17,500 | 18,750 | 52,500 | 61,250 | 62,500 | 66,250 | 227,500 | 311,250 |
| *Commercial* | 5,000 | 7,000 | 8,000 | 10,000 | 5,000 | 10,000 | 20,000 | 22,000 | 16,000 | 12,000 | 90,000 | 110,000 |
| *Prototypes* | 3,000 | 3,600 | 3,600 | 4,500 | 3,600 | 3,900 | 10,500 | 10,500 | 10,500 | 10,500 | 45,000 | 45,000 |
| Total | 24,750 | 24,600 | 28,600 | 29,500 | 26,100 | 32,650 | 83,000 | 93,750 | 89,000 | 88,750 | 362,500 | 466,250 |
| Total/month | 24,750 | 24,600 | 28,600 | 29,500 | 26,100 | 32,650 | 27,667 | 31,250 | 29,667 | 29,583 | 30,208 | 38,854 |

change in the process must be developed to allow more work to be completed in less space. This would suggest the need to decrease the lead time required to complete the work. This reduced lead time directly reduces the amount of work in process and the space required to store it. The management team has sufficient time to improve the processes and reduce the lead time so that future business levels can be accommodated in the current facility. If this is not possible, a larger facility is required to achieve the company's production plan. Either way, this is a very valuable planning tool since neither alternative can be completed in a short period of time.

Each planned resource has its own unique characteristics. Cash once consumed is no longer available for future use. Unconsumed cash can be held and used for future requirements. This resource can be added in small incremental amounts unlike plant square footage. Plant square footage numbers are meaningless on a cumulative annual basis. The square footage remains from one month to the next after use. Square footage is not easily added and subtracted. The addition of square footage is usually in large chunks of capacity. This resource is meaningful only in a monthly bucket amount. CNC capacity is much like square footage. Unused

**TABLE 2–5**

KC Manufacturing Resource Plan

| CNC Hours Required | | | | | | | | | | | |
|---|---|---|---|---|---|---|---|---|---|---|---|
| Product Groups | Jan | Feb | Mar | Apr | May | June | 3rd Q | 4th Q | 1st Q | 2nd Q | Next Year | Year After |
| RGB customer | 60 | 65 | 75 | 75 | 75 | 75 | 200 | 250 | 275 | 300 | 900 | 975 |
| ERT customer | 100 | 50 | 100 | 50 | 100 | 125 | 300 | 375 | 375 | 300 | 1,000 | 1,750 |
| QWR customer | 75 | 65 | 65 | 75 | 75 | 75 | 250 | 300 | 300 | 375 | 1,250 | 1,750 |
| Others | 100 | 100 | 100 | 100 | 100 | 100 | 300 | 300 | 300 | 350 | 1,400 | 1,750 |
| OEM Total | 335 | 280 | 340 | 300 | 350 | 375 | 1,050 | 1,225 | 1,250 | 1,325 | 4,550 | 6,225 |
| Commercial | 175 | 245 | 280 | 350 | 175 | 350 | 700 | 770 | 560 | 420 | 3,150 | 3,850 |
| Prototypes | 100 | 120 | 120 | 150 | 120 | 130 | 350 | 350 | 350 | 350 | 1,500 | 1,500 |
| Total | 610 | 645 | 740 | 800 | 645 | 855 | 2,100 | 2,345 | 2,160 | 2,095 | 9,200 | 11,575 |
| Hours available | 816 | 816 | 1,020 | 816 | 816 | 1,020 | 2,652 | 2,652 | 2,652 | 2,652 | 10,608 | 10,608 |

capacity cannot be rolled forward from one period to another as demonstrated in Table 2–5. Unlike cash, capacity not used to build product is not available for future use. This concept can be very difficult to grasp. Machine and labor capacity available from prior periods is zero. Once the day is gone, the capacity is too. Effective resource planning is more complex than just multiplying numbers and factors. The inherent characteristics of the resource type must also be considered.

For some resources, like CNC time, differences in capacity exist across the months due to the accounting periods defined as 4-4-5 weeks. Every third month has an extra week of time and therefore extra capacity. Realizing that capacity is not totally level is significant even at the top level of the production plan. If the plan is defined on a monthly basis, every third month should yield higher production since there is more capacity. Even considering the 4-4-5 cycle, in this particular example the production plan is providing an early warning that additional capacity is required for another CNC machine in two years. Like square footage, this resource's capacity must be added in large incremental pieces by the addition of new machines. When the numbers are evaluated, the addition of CNC capacity may begin sooner if the percentage utilization is too close to full capacity.

The historical accuracy of the forecast will be considered in the decision of when to purchase new equipment. If the forecast is historically conservative, the machines may be ordered sooner than the production plan may indicate. If the forecast is usually liberal, the decision to order the machines may wait.

The new equipment purchase decision is also dependent on the overall company strategy for competitiveness in the marketplace. Remember that when machines are running fairly close to capacity, the schedule of output is fairly stable. The incoming scheduled load closely matches the outgoing completions. Unfortunately, rarely will customer orders arrive in perfect balance to be run in the plant. Machines may not be scheduled at their best utilization if the order winner for the facility is rapid turnaround. Pursuing a strategy of short response lead time requires planning safety capacity. The amount of safety capacity is dependent on the variability of demand from the customer. Keep in mind that the production plan provides a rough-cut look at the projected load on each of these three key resources. Actual load and utilization will vary as customer orders arrive. This is where the detailed master production schedule comes into play. However, if the resources are not balanced at the production plan level, balancing them at a finer level is virtually impossible.

## DEVELOPING THE PRODUCTION PLAN—1, 2, 3

Developing a production plan can seem overwhelming. This section is an applied step-by-step "how to" approach that will result in a companywide production plan. The process of establishing the production plan must provide an opportunity for everyone to "buy into" the plan through involvement in its development. Because the production plan is such a valuable communications tool, many problems can be worked out in the development process that will prevent confusion later on the shop floor.

### Step 1: Identify Product Families

The first step in developing a production plan is the identification of product families. These are natural groupings of products made by the plant. They identify logical families for the products sold. Groupings can be by customer, market niche, or shared manufacturing process. This allows the plan to be developed at a higher level with significantly higher accuracy. Listen to how people in the company already refer to the products. Natural groups are identified by everyday use. To be the most useful, the production plan must fit the culture and language of the company. Product families are a natural evolution in most companies. For example, a plant making fan blades may have commercial products, OEM products, and custom products. A different plant in the sheet metal business may separate products into groups such as major customer accounts and custom parts. A plant making windows and doors may separate its products into doors and windows and then further into major product design groups such as sliders, stationary units, and custom products. These groups identify natural affinities for products because of the market niches served, shared manufacturing process, or major customer classification. When market niches are used as product groupings, the link to outside demand is enhanced. Efforts by marketing can be directed at enhancing the sales and interest of targeted market areas. The impact on production resources can be clearly seen from increasing sales in a target area.

Identifying natural groups due to shared manufacturing processes may allow for a simpler scheduling of the plant if the plant is organized by those processes. The plant-within-a-plant concept, where small subsets of the manufacturing process are identified and run as separate entities, can benefit from these product groupings. When major customers are used to identify product groupings, the production plan number then can be used to also forecast and monitor the level of business with key accounts. No matter how the groups are identified, they are then used for forecasting and planning purposes.

### Step 2: Select the Production Plan Unit of Measure

Most commonly the unit of measure for the forecast and the resulting production plan is sales revenue. These funds can then be related to critical pieces of capacity such as square footage, headcount, or a critical bottleneck machine utilization. The resources planned are determined by asking, What do we need to add to get more output? The answer is generally obvious to the company. The resources planned by the production plan are long lead items that take months or years to plan and acquire and are usually the ones that have had shortages in the past or other problems. The relationship between the dollars and the resources is developed by examining the history of the company. How many dollars of cash are required to support the business as the revenue level varies? What is the profitability per square foot of plant space? What is the utilization of equipment per dollar produced? These critical planning factors are used in developing the list of related resources in ratios to the production plan. This list of resources is also known as a bill of resources.

## Step 3: List Major Customers

Usually 80 to 90 percent of the products sold are to 10 to 20 percent of the customer base. Rather than spending time worrying about and forecasting all the little pieces, the law of large numbers dictates that getting the big piece close is good enough. Even though that might sound like heresy, a critical look must be taken at the cost of securing information compared to the value of that information. Asking these major customers what their expected purchase volumes are for the next year is an excellent way to start the production planning process. Having customer input directly into the forecasting process can greatly enhance the overall accuracy. Why guess at what the customer already has an idea about anyway? Remember that the main focus of the company is to profitably service the customer. Making them part of the production planning process can help both supplier and customer.

## Step 4: Obtain Historic Sales Data

These data should be defined by product family by customer for the last year (or two). Depending on the volatility of the market and the length of the product life cycle, one or two years of past data by customer for each product family can give great insights into past performance. This step takes the total business with each customer and further defines it into production families. Patterns in these detailed data can provide excellent insights for forecasting the future. The time bucket used for accumulating these data should be equal in length to the time buckets used for forecasting.

## Step 5: Project the Sales Data into the Future

Remember the three rules of using forecasts. First, forecasts are always wrong. Therefore, use every tool at your disposal to improve the odds. More detailed forecasting techniques are described in Chapter 3. Forecast the production plan in larger time buckets the farther out the forecast goes into the future. For most companies, the next month is planned by week followed by the next quarter by month. After the normal short-term planning horizon, use larger time buckets like quarters or years. The time planned into the future is directly dependent on the lead time of the critical resources.

## Step 6: Define Critical Resources and Calculate Requirements

Ask the question, What resource do we add to increase output? Do not settle for just the easy answers. Really dig into what is constraining production output. After these critical resources are defined, determine how much of each resource is required to produce each production family. Multiply the planned level of production by the quantity required, and an overall resource requirement plan is ready for review. Refer to Figures 2–1 through 2–6 for examples of how this identification and requirement calculation can be done.

## Step 7: Do a Validity Check

Ask the question that most people miss when working with computer tools: Does this make sense? The numbers developed in the previous steps are not necessarily correct just because a calculator or computer was used to develop them. Having more than one person look at the result can be a big help. Does the plan yield the overall financial results desired by the company? Is there a critical resource that has been forgotten? At this step, ask all the tough questions. Asking tough questions now can prevent tough problems later.

## Step 8: Have the Planning Meeting

After all the calculating and defining, the most important step in the process is to have a cross-functional meeting where key managers in the company get an opportunity to examine and participate in fine tuning the plan. Throwing the plan "over the wall" to the marketing and manufacturing people is a guarantee for sure failure. Having different functional areas intimately involved with the development of the plan right from step 1 will make this meeting very short. The production planning meeting is best held on a monthly basis. The next month is broken into weeks, and the planning horizon is rolled forward. Topics affecting the overall strategic performance of the company are discussed at this time. The overall financial performance is reviewed and any upcoming issues are identified. Everyone leaving the meeting should have a clear idea of past results, the plan for the future, and how the department fits into the plan.

The production plan is developed with the input of everyone affected by the plan. Typically the production planning meeting is held at least monthly to discuss the progress of the company towards its goals and update the plan for the future. A rolling horizon is maintained by adding the projected demand in future time buckets as the current demand becomes past business. At this meeting, key managers bring information concerning the performance of their department and how they contributed to the overall mission. The financial reports are reviewed, including actual sales dollars and the resulting profitability. Performance to strategic customer service measures is also discussed, such as percentage of on-time delivery, actual product mix demand, and general lead time response.

### Meeting Input Assignments

- **Marketing.** These people bring information about the expected future demands of current customers and possible additional markets that the company could address with either its current products or new products.
- **Engineering.** If the company is responsible for its own product development, the engineering department reports on the progress of current projects and shares ideas for future products.
- **Production.** This function brings information about process improvements and opportunities for upcoming capacity. The actual performance against plan is also reviewed.
- **Purchasing.** The purchasing function brings information about long lead time components and any identified strategic changes in the supplier market. This analysis

can include new suppliers in the market, new technologies available that can be utilized by the company, possible shortages of materials needed by the company, and price increases that will adversely impact the financial performance. Remember that 60 to 75 percent of the cost of goods sold is derived from material. The impact of the availability and cost of materials is key to successful overall financial performance.

The production plan is presented usually in terms of revenue dollars for each major product grouping. If the company makes only a few products in large volumes, the production plan can also be expressed as a rate of production for the product. An electronics company making battery chargers will use a production plan of the number of battery chargers per month, understanding that the actual master schedule of individual chargers built will be determined by actual customer orders received and desired stocking levels. Looking at production rates allows for common long lead time components and capacity to be planned. Even when the quantity of product is used for the production plan, the plan can be dollarized for budgeting and financial planning.

When these eight steps are followed, the result will be a high-quality production plan that can be communicated to everyone in the business. This top-level production plan is then used to drive the master schedule and, in turn, materials requirements planning. A well-defined architectural drawing drives all the building plans in the construction process. A well-developed production plan drives the rest of the planning process and helps determine which tools to use.

## SUMMARY

The commitment of all functions is required in the production planning process. A quicker and easier process would be for the chief executive to set sales targets and command each department to achieve the identified objective. Unfortunately, this kind of management by fear and intimidation is only successful for short periods of time. Long-term success depends on the full utilization of all resources, including each person's unique skills and abilities. Each department brings its contribution to the production plan just as a puzzle is constructed from many different pieces. When each piece is fitted into the whole, a picture emerges that is not evident when each piece is examined individually. The whole picture can then be supported by the resources required for implementation. Rather than having each function going its own way, the company moves more quickly towards its desired strategic goals and long-term success. Using the production plan, budgets can be developed using facts and actual plans rather than being based on a number of assumptions by the financial department. The result is better because more people had input into it. Since more people are part of the planning, they are also more committed to the implementation of the plan. The production plan is the company's handle on the aggregate business and makes other planning tools easier to use.

# ⑥ MASTER PRODUCTION SCHEDULE (MPS)

## INTRODUCTION

The Production Plan sets the overall production expectations for the company. Normally this plan is expressed in time buckets of a month, a quarter, or more. Manufacturing needs further detail when to begin the detailed scheduling process and acquisition of raw material. The Master Production Schedule (MPS) is derived from the Production Plan by breaking the Production Plan down into more detail. The Production Plan is usually stated in terms of dollars by product family. But manufacturing cannot build dollars or product families. Asking the factory to deliver dollars to the customer will be met with confusion and frustration. The Master Production Schedule answers the question, What should be built and when? This plan is then entered into the Material Requirements Planning system so that the availability of materials and capacity can be planned. The Master Production Schedule communicates expectations throughout the business. It translates the revenue and profit targets of senior management into understandable, achievable pieces for manufacturing. The Master Production Schedule is a statement of what can and will be created by the company.

Since the Master Production Schedule drives the detail planning system for materials and capacity, it should be challenging yet realistic. Having a past-due schedule that is twice or more the available capacity of the plant is not realistic. A realistic master schedule contains no past due work. As time moves ahead, uncompleted past-due work should be rescheduled to a realistic date. Having a past-due date driving the material planning system yields unrealistic due dates for upstream orders. Quickly everyone involved in the system learns to ignore the due dates, further increasing the problems. The Master Production Schedule should not be a management wish list of shipping volumes, nor a safe estimate from production of what can be easily completed. Rather, the Master Production Schedule should be an aggressive but realistic credible plan of what can be accomplished. The MPS represents a realistic consensus between production and sales and provides a companywide plan.

## INDEPENDENT AND DEPENDENT DEMAND

Product demand coming from outside the firm is called independent demand. A firm typically has little control over when and how much its customers order. Independent demand for finished goods is translated to dependent demand through the bills of material. Bills of material will be more fully discussed later, but for now they can be thought of as the recipe list of items needed to make the finished product. Dependent demand is calculated using the relationship of the dependent items to the independent demand end item. For example, independent demand for a bicycle will determine dependent demand for the wheels, frame, seat, and gears.

### Example

A partial bill of material for a bike includes two wheels, one frame, one seat, and one set of gears. If a customer places an order for 100 bicycles, this is independent demand. The company would then require 200 wheels, 100 frames, 100 seats, and 100 gears as dependent demand. The demand for the wheels, frames, seats, and gears is dependent on the outside demand for bicycles.

Individual parts can have both independent and dependent demands. For example, if the bicycle wheels were also sold as a separate service part, they would have independent demand in addition to the dependent demand. If 75 individual tires would be sold as service parts, the total demand for wheels is 275. Two hundred tires are needed to build the 100 bicycles and 75 will be shipped separately. The Master Production Schedule is the tool developed to respond to independent demands. It fits all the demands together like a puzzle and balances the demands with available capacity. This top-level plan then drives the material planning system. Material Requirements Planning is the tool that calculates all dependent demand.

## UNDERSTANDING LEAD TIME

To aid in planning the procurement functions, the Master Production Schedule must cover a length of time that is at least as long as the cumulative lead time. A common error is to plan into the future only the length of the longest purchased part lead time. This does not allow any time for conversion of the parts into finished goods nor shipment to the customer. Regardless of the type of business—make to order, make to stock, or assemble to order— the Master Production Schedule must look out at least as long as the *total* cumulative lead time to be effective. Estimated lead times would seem like an easy question. However, total lead time includes some unexpected factors. This "easy question" can be difficult to estimate accurately. Total cumulative lead time includes:

• **Development time.** This is the amount of time required to develop and define a product. It can vary significantly by product type. If the product is a minor modification or derivative of an old product, the time could be very short. However, if new technology is being developed, the time can be very long. If the company is responsible for developing its own products, the lead time for this function must be included in the MPS planning horizon. The project manager rule is that whatever development lead time is estimated, double it to be safe (and then add a 10 percent safety factor). This ultraconservative approach can adversely impact the company by making it noncompetitive in the market due to long lead time and lack of responsiveness. The ability to quickly develop and bring products to the market can be a core success strategy for a business. The estimation of the development time should be as realistic as possible.

- **Purchasing time.** Purchasing lead time is the amount of time required to place a purchase order from a supplier. This lead time includes the time required to know what parts are needed and do the paperwork to order them. Depending on the environment, this time can be very short or very long. If competitive quoting is used before ordering parts, the purchasing time can stretch to weeks. One of the advantages of supplier partnerships is that significantly less time is used defining needs and ordering the correct parts. All the overhead required in the quoting and ordering function provides little value to the overall process. These functions merely add cost. The mission of the procurement function is to spend the company's money wisely. Purchasing provides the right parts, at the right time, at the right cost. Reducing the time and effort devoted to these functions benefits the company directly and the external customer indirectly. The lead time associated with preparing and placing the order is often overlooked and can be a critical lead time factor.

- **Planning frequency.** Many companies only run their Material Requirements Planning system replanning once per week. This batch approach to planning adds lead time to the overall lead time since the parts are only planned on an infrequent basis. If a need arises for the part the day after the MRP planning was run, almost an entire week is added to the total lead time before this need can be addressed. This planning time can be a significant barrier to reduction of overall lead times. Longer lead times result in higher levels of inventory. Reducing lead times has a direct impact on overall inventory levels.

- **Supplier lead time.** This portion of lead time is usually the quoted time from the supplier to get the part. Care must be taken to determine if the quoted lead time includes transportation time to the destination. Depending on the location of the supplier, this factor alone may be many times greater than the fabrication time at the supplier. Supplier lead times can be extremely dynamic. The electronics industry is notorious for rapidly changing lead times and widely varying component availability. One week an item might be found in stock. The next week when placing an order, the buyer might find that lead times have expanded to 18 weeks and the item is on allocation. Staying in close contact with suppliers is very important in obtaining early warnings of changing lead times.

• **Transportation time.** Another lead time component is the transportation time to get the part from the origin to the destination. Extreme variability can occur as distances become greater. Having a supplier across town tends to result in more reliable lead times than having a supplier halfway around the world. The mode of transportation can also add variability. Air shipments tend to be more reliable, while shipments by boat can be extremely variable. If the raw materials are being shipped by an intermodal process (ship to train to truck, for example), the variability can be even greater. Reliability of transportation time is a key reason why local suppliers are favored by many businesses. Remember that one of the functions of inventory is to cover variability. If there is a risk that the ship will be late or weather will interfere with the transportation of parts, the natural reaction is to carry increased inventory.

• **Receipt time.** This time can also be consequential depending on the process used for receiving parts. If every shipment must be validated for count and specifications, the receiving inspection area will consume a significant amount of time and resources. This area can become the bottleneck of the procurement process. Momentous effort is expended to prioritize the incoming material to support the conversion process. Similar to the process of detailed quoting for each order, the value of receiving inspection is questionable. The additional work required to inspect parts and validate counts for all incoming parts requires significant resources. In reality, only 15 to 20 percent of the incoming supplies will have problems. These are the only parts that should be subjected to additional work. Quickly a track record is established for suppliers. The receiving people know which suppliers are counting and quality challenged. Instead of increasing the lead time and efforts for all parts, focus on these problem parts and suppliers.

• **Fabrication time.** This is the amount of time required to convert the purchased items into finished goods for shipment to the customer. This part of lead time includes the time required to know what is going to be built, gather all required parts, actually build the product, transact the completion to the formal inventory system, and pack it for the customer. The time required for paperwork documenting the production process may exceed the time required to build the parts. Both factors must be included in estimating this lead time.

- **Order fulfillment time.** This is the time from the receipt of the customer's order to the shipment of the part. Depending on the production environment, this time can include a number of the previous lead time components for a make-to-order company or can be added to the end of the fabrication time for a make-to-stock company.

The important thing to remember about the different components of lead time is that each can make a big difference in the overall competitiveness of the company. Customers expect quick response and short planning horizons. The long lead times associated with some parts and resources are in direct conflict with the market direction. If the Master Production Schedule horizon is cut short, the purchasing department will be the first to know and will always be in a state of panic and expediting. The expectations of the customer base are towards ever improving lead time response. Some companies have chosen to accomplish this by making product to inventory, while others have reduced the actual cumulative lead time and service the customer within their expectations without building finished goods to be available off the shelf.

Lead time and inventory levels are similar. Each will increase in response to unplanned events. Both are insurance policies against the unknown or undependable. As competitive factors continue to change, it is a safe bet that the increased customer expectations for shorter lead times will continue. The shorter lead times have a dramatic effect on the process of master scheduling. How companies choose to manage their external demands from the customer are linked to the overall company strategy. Determining what parts to schedule in the Master Production Schedule for the make-to-stock company can be accomplished through forecasting. The Production Plan communicates the product family expectations in total, and the Master Production Schedule breaks this into further detail by product. If this finer detail is unknown at the beginning of the planning time horizon, forecasting must be used.

## DEVELOPING THE FORECAST

In many companies, the Master Production Schedule horizon is longer than firmly booked business due to long lead components and resources. In this situation, forecasting must be used to provide a basis for the future Master Production Schedule. Remember from Chapter 2 that the three basic rules of forecasting are:

1. The forecast is always wrong.
2. The forecast is less accurate further in the future.
3. The forecast is less accurate in finer detail.

However, forecasts usually pay dividends in excess of their cost to develop. A forecast that is 20 percent wrong is still 80 percent right. Not forecasting will always be 100 percent wrong.

Forecasting can take two major forms, qualitative and quantitative. Qualitative forecasting is often a gut feel opinion of what sales will be. By default, every company has used this method of forecasting. The qualitative method is most commonly used because there is a general lack of understanding about how to do quantitative forecasting. Quantitative forecasting uses numbers to calculate a reasonable estimate for demand. A phobia about doing numerical calculations also inhibits the use of quantitative forecasting for many people. Today the formulae only need to be defined once. After that the computer makes easy work out of the calculations. Some simple but commonly used quantitative tools for forecasting independent demands follow.

### Simple Moving Average

This is the simplest, most commonly used method of forecasting. The last few periods of actual demand data are added and then averaged. The result is used as the future forecast. The advantage of this method is that it is easy to understand and compute. The disadvantage is that it is rarely the best solution. The best use of simple moving average is for relatively stable data. The number of periods that are chosen to average will determine the responsiveness of the forecast. Including more periods means the forecast will respond more slowly to the changes in the data. Fewer periods mean that the forecast will respond more quickly to data changes.

**Example**
Most recent sales: 120, 125, 135.
Forecast for next period: (120 + 125 + 135)/3 = 126.6 or 127.
However, the sales for next month were really 140.
Forecast for next period: (125 + 135 + 140)/3 = 133.3 or 134.

The forecast was rounded up even though arithmetic rules would state that the number should be 133. When any remainder is left, the number is always rounded up. Since partial parts are not an option, the best choice is to always increase the forecast by one unit.

The most recent periods are simply added and averaged to obtain the forecast for the next period. Another disadvantage is that this only provides a forecast one period into the future. The downside of this method of forecasting severely limits its application, but simple moving average is commonly used because it is simple to understand and calculate.

## Weighted Moving Average

This method is an improvement on the simple moving average. Weighted moving average takes advantage of the fact that the most recent past is usually a better predictor of the future than the remote past. The weights are at the discretion of the forecaster. The total of all the weights must equal 1.0. Most commonly used weights are 0.7 and 0.3 or 0.5, 0.3, and 0.2. Important things to remember are that the heaviest weight goes to the most recent history and that all weights must add up to 1.0.

Using the same data of the simple moving average example but changing the forecasting method results in a very different answer.

**Example**
Forecast for next month (using the first three months of data) would be (0.2)(120) + (0.3)(125) + (0.5)(135) = 129.

Assume that the actual demand for the previously forecasted month was 140. The forecast for next month would be (0.2)(125) + (0.3)(135) + (0.5)(140) = 135.5 or 136.

The weighted average is more responsive than the simple average. The forecast picked up the change in the demand and increased the forecast accordingly. More weight put on the most recent history causes the forecast to react even more strongly. If the weights used are changed, the answer changes dramatically.

**Example—Two-period Weighted Moving Average**
Forecast for the same two periods would be (.3)(125) + (.7)(135) = 132.

Compare this to the three-period simple moving average answer (127) or the three-period weighted moving average (129). The fewer the number of periods used, the more responsive the forecast. The next period experiences the same phenomenon when the forecast is calculated. (.3)(135) + (.7)(140) = 138.5 or 139.

With just a few data points and two simple forecasting techniques, three very different answers have been calculated. Which one is right? The answer is that they all are! The best tool for the job is one that fits the data patterns best. Sometimes there is a strong pattern to the data. One of the strongest patterns is trend.

## Trend Analysis

Trend analysis acknowledges that the sales of an item can sometimes be predicted by the passage of time. The ever increasing sales over time is the most common application of this forecast technique. The calculation of the forecast can be done either  by simply looking at the graph or by calculating a trend line. Another method is to use a spreadsheet to find the line of best fit. When trend is suspected, the best way to confirm the impression is to graph the data. Remember that "a picture is worth a thousand words." In the graph in Figure 3–1, the next logical forecast for month five would be greater than 140. The forecast could then be set at 145 with confidence. Another way to calculate the trend is to take the end pointand the beginning point and calculate the average trend.

**FIGURE 3–1**

Historical Demand

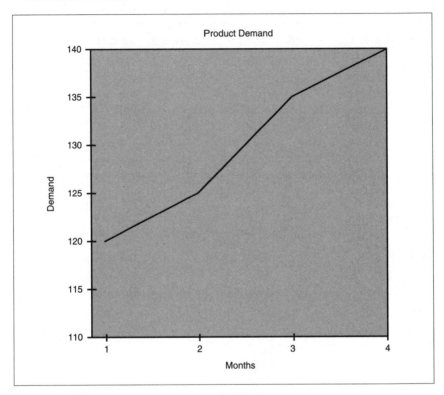

**Example**
Trend = (end point – beginning)/number of periods.
Trend = (140 – 120)/3 = 6.67.
Forecast = end point + trend.
Forecast = 140 + 6.67 = 147

On a spreadsheet, the best fit line gave the result of 147.5 or 148. The difference between the naïve method (145), the average trend method (147), and the more precisely calculated method using a spreadsheet (148) is minimal. With a different set of data, the results of these three methods of calculating trend may not be as close. The best initial tool to use with any method is the graph. Looking at a graphical representation of the data can reveal many insights that are not evident in the data table.

## Seasonality

Some businesses are seasonal. Examples of seasonal businesses are manufacturers of snowmobiles, snow skis, water skis, and lawn mowers. Items are built all year that are used mainly during one period of the year. This pattern of consumption tends to be the same year after year. Using seasonality forecasting tools for seasonal products results in higher accuracy than any of the tools described so far. The advantage of using seasonality is that a recognizable pattern is used for forecasting the data. The pattern can be calculated rather precisely. Only the average change in baseline from year to year must be forecast.

### Product Sales

| Quarter | Year 1 | Year 2 |
|---------|--------|--------|
| 1 | 50 | 60 |
| 2 | 75 | 90 |
| 3 | 62 | 75 |
| 4 | 45 | 52 |

Assume that the previous table contains the previous two years of sales data. Once again the data are graphed and the seasonality of the demand is very apparent. There is an increase in sales during the second quarter, and sales decline during the final quarter of the year. In addition, the product has increased in sales between year 1 and year 2. Not only does the product appear to experience seasonality, but a trend is also evident. This is graphically represented in Figure 3–2. The forecast must take into account both phenomena. To calculate the forecast, first the seasonality is determined.

### Product Sales

| | | | Step 1 | Step 2 | Step 3 |
|---------|--------|--------|--------|--------|----------|
| Quarter | Year 1 | Year 2 | Total | Index | Forecast |
| 1 | 50 | 60 | 110 | 0.86 | 69 |
| 2 | 75 | 90 | 165 | 1.30 | 104 |
| 3 | 62 | 75 | 137 | 1.08 | 86 |
| 4 | 45 | 52 | 97 | 0.76 | 61 |
| Average | 58 | 69.25 | 127.25 | 4.00 | 80 |

**FIGURE   3–2**

Seasonal Demand

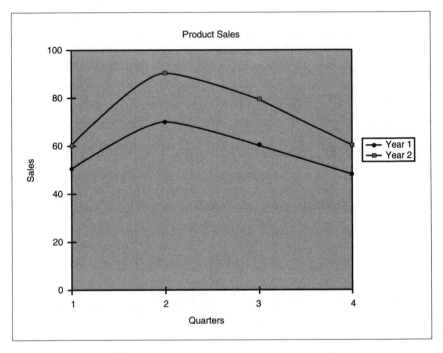

**Step 1:** To calculate the seasonality, the two years are totaled. This is displayed in the column labeled step 1. The simple average is then calculated for this total. The number 127.25 is not indicative of any sales projection, but it is a necessary step in the computation.

**Step 2:** The next step is to take the average of the totals (127.25) and divide it back into the total for each quarter. This results in the numbers displayed in the column marked step 2. The first entry is 110/127.25 = .86. The display has been rounded to two decimal points for clarity. These index weights should add to the total number of periods used for indexing, four. The meaning of these numbers is that in the first quarter, typically only 86 percent of average sales is experienced. The second quarter is greater than average with an index of 1.30. If the demand pattern were level each quarter, the indexes would all equal one.

Since the data are seasonal, these weights are essential in the forecasting process. If only a simple average were used, sales would look very bad in the first quarter, great in the second and third quarters, and very bad again in the fourth quarter. Actions could be taken that are unnecessary to correct an expected fluctuation in demand.

**Step 3:** The next step is to forecast the average sales per quarter for the next year. Since the first year's average is 58 per quarter and the next year's average is 69.25 per quarter, a trend of 11 units per quarter is used. This results in an average forecast of 80 per quarter (69 + 11). But, since the data are obviously seasonal, this forecast must be seasonalized into the appropriate quarters. This projection is multiplied by the seasonality factors calculated in step 2. The forecast for next year is displayed in the column marked step 3.

The advantage of using a seasonalized forecast is that unusual trends can be identified sooner. For example, if sales during the first quarter are 80, the forecaster suspects that possibly sales may be higher than expected for the year since only 69 were expected to be sold. On the other hand, if the sales for the first quarter are 68, this is accepted as a normal fluctuation. The sales in the first quarter typically are less than the average. Seasonality allows the calculation of patterns of demand and removes this known entity from interfering with the real forecast issues.

## Selecting a Method

Using a combination of these methods can result in sophisticated forecasting models capable of high levels of responsiveness and accuracy. Selecting which tool to use can seem confusing. Actually, the selection is made by using different possible methods on demand data that are already known. The different methods are used to forecast results that are then compared to known actual demand. After one calculates the error using these possible forecast methods, a selection can be made based on the smallest error. Based on similar logic that past demand can predict future demand, the method that most accurately projects known historical demand data should best forecast future unknown demand. A forecaster might take actual data from two years ago and test several methods to forecast last year's sales. The forecaster would then compare the forecast to last year's actual sales. The method that most accurately forecast actual sales would be selected for future forecasting. Software packages are available that automatically do these calculations and best fit the forecasting method to the data. However, at the current time these forecasting packages can cost more than the entire integrated planning system. If higher forecast accuracy is needed than can be developed with these simple tools, perhaps the software investment is worthwhile.

## EVALUATING AND USING THE FORECAST

Since forecasts are at best an estimate of the future, measuring and managing the amount and type of error is important to manage effectively. Some tools used to measure forecast accuracy are error, bias, and standard error.

### Error

This is the simplest of the accuracy measures. Error is calculated by subtracting the forecast from the actual number. When all the error numbers are added together (cumulative error) and the pluses and minuses are allowed to cancel each other out, a rough measure of accuracy can be obtained. This error measure is calculated for each forecasted part individually. A meaningful common unit of measure such as dollars must be used to forecast groups of parts.

Actual Sales Compared to Forecast

| Quarter | Actual | Forecast | Error |
|---------|--------|----------|-------|
| 1 | 69 | 72 | −3 |
| 2 | 104 | 101 | 3 |
| 3 | 86 | 82 | 4 |
| 4 | 61 | 59 | 2 |

Cumulative error: 6

The closer the number is to zero, the better the forecast. If the total error is positive, the conclusion is that the forecast has been consistently too low. If the total error is negative, the forecast has been consistently too high. In this example, the forecast has been cumulatively too low. Adjustments can be made based on the size and direction of the total error. Unfortunately, one weakness is that the cumulative effect depends on where the starting point is identified. If the error is calculated for a product group, the accuracy should be better because of the larger grouping. Remember the third rule of forecasting, that forecasts are better for higher consolidations of data. The disadvantage is that the factory cannot build dollars. At some point the dollars must be translated into a unique item that can be built. Do not select a forecasting method and grouping just to enhance accuracy; the forecast must also be useful when completed.

## Bias

Bias answers the question of the cumulative starting point by averaging the error. Bias is calculated by adding all the errors and dividing by the number of errors that were added.

Bias Calculation—Actual Sales Compared to Forecast

| Quarter | Actual | Forecast | Error |
|---------|--------|----------|-------|
| 1 | 69 | 72 | −3 |
| 2 | 104 | 101 | 3 |
| 3 | 86 | 82 | 4 |
| 4 | 61 | 59 | 2 |
| | | Cumulative error: 6 | |
| | | **Bias**     6/4 = 1.5 | |

Just like error, if the bias is positive, the forecast has been too low, on average. If the bias is negative, the forecast has been too high, on average. In this example, the forecast has been too low, on average. The closer the bias is to zero means that the forecast, on average, is more precise. The problem with averages is that when each period is examined, the amount of error could be huge, but the errors could average out in the end. A seasonal demand pattern could have a very small error or bias over the course of the year but be way off in any one month or quarter. From a real-world approach, forecast accuracy is required for each period, not just over a long period on average. This variability of demand is the main cause behind safety stock inventory in the operation. The best way to assess the real accuracy of the forecast is to use the standard error.

## Standard Error

The disadvantage of the error and bias is that the positive and negative errors can cancel out each other. These can both be zero, and the forecast can swing widely. The usefulness of this highly variable forecast is questionable. The effect on customer service and inventory levels is devastating. Either there is insufficient inventory to service demand or excess inventory on hand. When the forecast is less than demand, the customer could be asked to wait. The customer may not be willing to wait and will take the business to another supplier that can supply the item when requested. This effect can severely impact a make-to-stock company. In a make-to-stock company, more items are forecast individually, and the customer expects a rapid order fulfillment time—the worst of both worlds. When the forecast is more than demand, critical resources are spent building the wrong items. The standard error does not allow the pluses and minuses to cancel out each other.

The benefit of the standard error is that the dispersion of the forecast is calculated. Standard error assesses the variability of the forecast error. Variability is the gremlin of any process. When a process is extremely reliable, no inventory or excess capacity is needed. When a process is extremely variable, safety inventory or capacity is used to buffer against unexpected events. Forecasts are estimates of the unknown. The more reliable these estimates are, the less safety inventory and capacity are required to provide excellent customer service. Even though the forecast may jump around due to expected events like seasonality and promotions, if these changes can be forecasted accurately, safety stock is not required.

Sales Standard Error Calculations

| Month | Forecast | Actual | Error | Step 1 Error Squared |
|---|---|---|---|---|
| 1 | 100 | 97 | −3 | 9 |
| 2 | 100 | 110 | 10 | 100 |
| 3 | 100 | 102 | 2 | 4 |
| 4 | 100 | 105 | 5 | 25 |
| 5 | 100 | 115 | 15 | 225 |
| 6 | 100 | 103 | 3 | 9 |
| 7 | 100 | 124 | 24 | 576 |
| 8 | 100 | 130 | 30 | 900 |
| 9 | 100 | 100 | 0 | 0 |
| 10 | 100 | 103 | 3 | 9 |
| 11 | 100 | 120 | 20 | 400 |
| 12 | 100 | 122 | 22 | 484 |

Total: 2741 **Step 2**

Standard error: 15.79 **Step 3**

**Step 1:** The standard error is calculated by first squaring all the errors (multiply the error by itself).

**Step 2:** Add the squared errors together.

**Step 3:** The next step divides the cumulative error by the number of data points minus one, and then the square root is taken to find the standard error. At first glance this process looks confusing and difficult. If many standard errors have to be calculated manually, it is. Fortunately, even the most rudimentary spreadsheet software can calculate the standard error for a column of numbers in one simple formula. The real usefulness for this tool is in its application. The smaller the standard error, the better the forecast.

The information captured in the standard error affects many areas of customer service and forecasting. Once the standard error is known, this number can be used to calculate the safety stock required to maintain a desired level of customer service.

## Safety Stock

Traditionally, companies use qualitative judgment to determine safety stocks. Favorite rules are to keep one month supply extra or a fixed quantity always in stock. Rarely does this method give the desired service level. With the standard error method, the safety stock is a more realistic representation of the true demand variation. A customer service level can be chosen, and the safety stock required to deliver that level of expected customer service can be calculated—a far better method than throwing the dart at the board or just picking a number.

The following safety stock levels were developed by multiplying the standard error by the appropriate safety factor. These safety factors can be found in any statistics book in a Z-value table. A few commonly used factors are provided.

| Desired Customer Service Level | Safety Factor |
| --- | --- |
| 90% | 1.28 |
| 95 | 1.65 |
| 98 | 2.05 |
| 99 | 2.33 |
| 99.999999 | 4.00 |

In the example used, the safety stocks required for each desired level of customer service are listed below using the standard error calculated earlier.

| Desired Customer Service Level | Safety Stock Required |
| --- | --- |
| 90% | 20 |
| 95 | 26 |
| 98 | 32 |
| 99 | 37 |
| 99.99 | 63 |

With this quantitative information, a realistic quantitative management decision can be made. A comparison can be made of the cost of carrying 37 parts in safety stock to provide 99 percent customer service compared to 20 parts and only 90 percent service. Depending on the cost of the part, this could mean a notable investment. The overall forecasting process can be measured by the standard error over time. Even though the forecast is never expected to be perfectly accurate, the reduction in standard error will show how the forecast has improved. Any improvement in the level of forecasting accuracy positively impacts the level of safety stock required. The less error in the forecasting process means less required safety stock to service the customer.

With this small toolbox of mathematical forecasting tools, the master scheduler, in cooperation with the marketing and sales department, can develop a master schedule to fulfill the product demands. The master schedule is a realistic statement of what can and will be built and looks out at least as long as the cumulative lead time. The master schedule may be a big wall chart, white board, or a sophisticated computer model. The goal is to communicate the overall needs of the customer and how they will be serviced by the company. The master schedule is the beginning of the tactical plans.

## DEVELOPING THE MASTER SCHEDULE

The master scheduler can be thought of as a master puzzle assembler. This person takes independent product demand from all sources and fits the labor and parts requirements into a schedule that utilizes plant capacity with a level load. Care is taken not to overload or underload any of the work centers while simultaneously managing the inventory and servicing the customer. When it all comes together, it can look a bit like magic. Computer software companies are attempting to develop expert systems that will do this kind of balancing automatically. But not one expert system has been developed at an affordable price that can compare to the human scheduler. The basic steps for developing the master schedule follow.

### Step 1: Determine the Production Environment

Different production strategies can be used for responding to customer orders. A company can be "make to stock," "make to order," "engineer to order," or "assemble to order." How the master schedule is developed depends on the strategy for production.

- *Make to stock.* In a make-to-stock company, the customer expects instant fulfillment of its order from an existing inventory. The master scheduler considers all independent demand items and schedules production based on the forecast of future sales. Forecasts are done for each of the end items possible in the plant. The number of independent end items is limited. A customer must choose from one of the predefined items available for sale. A typical make-to-stock company takes many dependent demand components and converts them into significantly fewer independent demand items. The order fulfillment time is very short. Any desired changes in the inventory of independent demand items must be included in the Master Production Schedule. If the inventory is planned to increase, the scheduler must schedule that increased production. If the inventory is planned to decrease, the appropriate adjustment is made in the schedule. The Master Production Schedule is the same as the final assembly schedule in the make-to-stock company.

- *Make to order.* In a make-to-order company, production is not started until the customer order is received. Small businesses typically pursue this strategy. The customer is capable of ordering an infinite number of items using the flexible processes available in the plant. Forecasts focus on critical resources and common raw materials rather than independent demand items. The final assembly schedule prioritizes end item orders using available capacity. Financial resources are not invested in materials until there is a relatively high certainty of winning the order. The order fulfillment time for the make-to-order strategy is typically longer than make to stock. Another factor for the scheduler to consider is the desired change in backlog. Backlog is customer orders that have been received but are not yet shipped. If the plan is to increase backlog, the Master Production Schedule must be less than the rate of incoming orders. Conversely, if the desire is to decrease backlog, a higher level of output must be scheduled. The concern in the make-to-order company is good utilization of the company's flexible resources. Customer orders tend to arrive in such a manner that does not level load the plant. The master scheduler must prioritize and schedule orders in such a manner to minimize disruption in the plant and maximize customer service.

- *Engineer to order.* The engineer-to-order company develops a product that meets the specifications and intent of the customer. The company is responsible for the design, development, and production of the final product. The order fulfillment time is longest in this type of company. Typically, one of the most critical resources in the company that requires effective closed-loop planning is engineering. This department can quickly become the bottleneck for the entire company's growth. Addition of resources to this area can take a relatively long time to be fully effective. The master scheduler is not only concerned with production, but also with the design area. Engineering backlog must be managed separately but integrated to be most effective.

- *Assemble to order.* This production strategy is a combination of the make-to-order and make-to-stock approaches. A forecast is done for a relatively small number of common semifinished goods. These items can then be combined in a number of different ways depending on the customer's wishes. This strategy allows the customer to have more flexibility in defining the final configuration of the product but also allows quick response to its order. The master schedule is defined for semifinished items that will be made to stock. A final assembly schedule is developed as actual customer orders arrive and the final product is fully defined. The same concerns about inventory exist for the semifinished items as in the make-to-stock strategy. The Master Production Schedule must consider any desired changes to semifinished inventory levels. At the same time, the schedule for final assembly must consider any desired changes to the backlog, similar to the make-to-order strategy.

## Step 2: Calculate Total Demand

The Master Production Schedule must consider all the demands. Demand can come from a variety of sources. If the company decides to use a mix of the production strategies, the total demand can be challenging to fully quantify. Remember to consider internal as well as external demand for products. This does not mean that forecasts or estimates need to be made for dependent demand. MRP will calculate this type of demand. The total demand is only independent demand. Commonly missed demand sources are production development, engineering requirements, and sales samples.

## Step 3: Determine Critical Resources and Calculate Loads

Similar to the Production Planning process, the validity of the Master Production Schedule must be checked against capacity. The bottleneck resource of the plant will determine the overall throughput. This resource is critical to identify and utilize in a way that enhances profitability. This plan will further detail the capacity load on critical resources. Figure 3–3 shows the results of a critical resource load and capacity comparison.

The assembly area is drastically overloaded in the week of 12/31 and underloaded in all the weeks prior to and after this crisis week. An effective master scheduler would examine

**FIGURE  3–3**

Capacity Requirements Planning—Work Center Loading

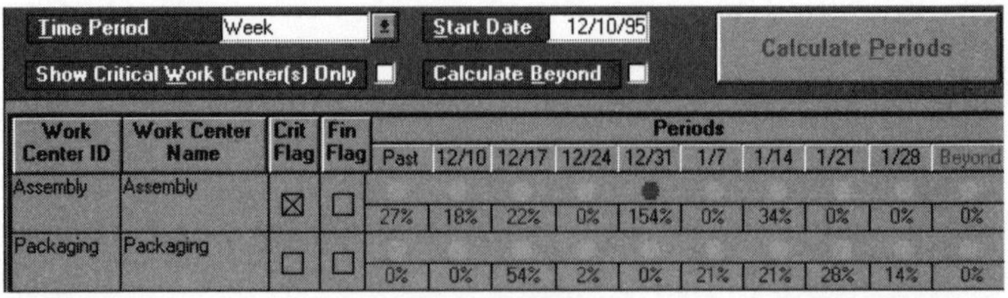

| Work Center ID | Work Center Name | Crit Flag | Fin Flag | Past | 12/10 | 12/17 | 12/24 | 12/31 | 1/7 | 1/14 | 1/21 | 1/28 | Beyond |
|---|---|---|---|---|---|---|---|---|---|---|---|---|---|
| Assembly | Assembly | ☒ | ☐ | 27% | 18% | 22% | 0% | 154% | 0% | 34% | 0% | 0% | 0% |
| Packaging | Packaging | ☐ | ☐ | 0% | 0% | 54% | 2% | 0% | 21% | 21% | 28% | 14% | 0% |

this load and attempt to reschedule orders to earlier and later weeks to result in a more even load. This kind of visibility when calculated into the future provides an exceptional opportunity for proactive planning. Even with only the three weeks advance notice in Figure 3–3, the scheduler can develop a plan to solve the problem before the problem arrives. Once the scheduler determines a feasible solution, the necessary changes are made in the formal system to reflect this plan. The Material Requirements Planning system can then calculate the needed material and capacity to accomplish the plan. These calculations and system visibility is one of the benefits of an integrated MRP system implementation. The purchasing and production functions no longer have to second guess each other. There is one plan and everyone is working to it.

## Step 4: Measure Results

A key measure for the business is the ability to perform to the master schedule. Promises to customers and detailed budgets are prepared using this critical plan. Credibility of the plan is a key tool in the overall usage of the formal system. Different philosophies exist on measuring the results of the Master Production Schedule. One method is to calculate the Master Production Schedule accuracy similar to the calculation of inventory record accuracy. Each item is considered on its own, and then the number of items shipped on schedule are divided by the total number of items for an overall master schedule percentage accuracy. The disadvantage of this method is that line items with high values are considered with the same priority as low-value items. Another method is to calculate the percentage of total dollars shipped on schedule. The disadvantage here is that the focus can shift easily to manipulating the measure by ensuring the shipment of only high-dollar items. The low-value items that are neglected in the process can be critical to the customer. In an effort to prevent this manipulation of the data, many companies track the performance to the MPS using both methods. The method selected for measuring master schedule performance must fit the unique needs of the business, and it must be utilized consistently.

## SUMMARY

The Master Production Schedule is the anticipated build schedule for the plant. This plan translates the financial plans of the Production Plan into a detailed manufacturing plan by item. The Master Production Schedule answers, What will be built, how much will be built, and when will it be built? For a make-to-stock company, detailed item forecasting may be needed to determine the quantity of individual parts that should be scheduled. This plan in turn drives Material Requirements Planning. Purchasing and manufacturing work together to achieve this plan. Purchases of raw material are made to support the scheduled production. Priorities are established through the Master Production Schedule for scarce resources. This plan is kept realistic by validating the schedule against a rough-cut capacity plan. The critical junction of strategy and tactics must be realistic for the success of the overall formal planning system.

# 4

# BILLS OF MATERIAL AND RESOURCES

## INTRODUCTION

The toolbox for defining bills of material provides many choices and options to represent the configuration of the products. Just like construction, having the right tools makes the whole job easier and quicker. Choosing the right tool for the bill of material job enhances overall utilization and accuracy and improves the results of the MRP system. Usually the number of chief engineers a company has had can be determined by looking at the number of different ways bills of material have been structured. The topic of bill of material structuring usually evokes strong feelings from everyone in the organization who uses these tools. Since bills of material are used for costing, scheduling, product definition, work orders, and many other functions, almost everyone in the organization has an opinion. Properly structured bills of material make the job easy, while improper structures can create problems, extra work, and errors.

Bills of material are a list of all the items required to make another part. The top-end item is called the parent item, and the items that are required to make the parent item are called components. The quantity on the bill of material for each component is sufficient to make one of the parent parts.

**Examples of Bills of Material**

| Bicycle | 1 ea | Parent |
|---|---|---|
| • Wheels | 2 ea | Component |
| • Seat | 1 ea | Component |
| • Handlebars | 1 ea | Component |
| • Gears | 1 ea | Component |
| | | |
| Lamp | 1 ea | Parent |
| • Bulb | 1 ea | Component |
| • Socket base | 1 ea | Component |
| • Shade | 1 ea | Component |
| • Base | 1 ea | Component |
| • Electrical Cord | 6 ft | Component |

We normally think in term of bills of material without realizing it. We cook from recipes that are bills of material for food. Recipes are doubled or halved by adjusting each item on the ingredient list by the same factor. This is the same as changing a lot size for a manufactured product. We assemble our tools and raw materials for our hobbies—another bill of material. Daily we schedule different tasks at different times using a calendar or electronic scheduling device—a bill of resources, another version of a bill of material. This bill of material logic allows us to think of groups of parts belonging to other parts or assemblies. All items on the bill of material are needed to complete the parent item.

Bills of material are the core of an MRP system. The relationship of component items to parent finished goods in conjunction with the master production schedule allows the requirements for the component goods to be calculated exactly rather than forecasted incorrectly. There is no need to guess how many bicycle wheels are required when the number of bikes that will be built is known. If the master production schedule calls for 100 bikes, 200 wheels are needed to complete the order.

The bills of material are used by virtually everyone in the organization. Frequently, different areas will develop and maintain their own bills of material. The inconsistency in this approach is that each area believes that its bill of material is the correct one. The reality is that often none of the bills accurately reflects all the materials and resources used. People who would not dream of having multiple policies and procedures for each functional area support having multiple bills of material in the company. The bill of material is a company document just like company policies and procedures. Only one version should be used by everyone in the company. Each functional group may use it for different purposes, but one definition is required. The bill of material is like a language definition. We all use it for different purposes, but one common standard is needed for effective communication.

## USES OF BILLS OF MATERIAL AND RESOURCES

### Defining Products and Resource Needs

Engineers use bills of material to define products and their components. The unique item number identification used may be the same as the drawing number. This is not a system requirement. Many companies use item numbers different from the drawing number. Depending on the process for creating drawings, the engineer may use one drawing to describe multiple parts. The bill of material may be defined as part of the engineering drawing development. Having the drawing number match or not match the bill of material is not critical for success. Modern systems allow the tracking of the unique item identification and the corresponding drawing number. What really matters is that the bill of material provides sufficient information to work down the entire product definition tree and communicate what is required to complete the product. Many software packages allow entry of drawing numbers on the same record as the part number. This allows one drawing to exist for many unique part numbers. The bill of material would use the unique part identifier.

> **Example**
> Our company assembles felt tip markers. The components for the marker are case, top, inked felt piece, and plug. Engineering could structure each of the subassemblies as a part number. Manufacturing knows it would not make sense to put the case-felt subassembly in stock because it would dry out and be useless.

Manufacturing could plan the case-felt subassembly as a phantom and assemble the finished unit in one assembly process, with no interruption. The result is a quality product and one bill of material for the company, usable by everyone.

Critical resources are placed into the bill of resources so that visibility of overall requirements can be calculated and managed. The question What do we need to add to get more output? is essential to manufacturing planning for staffing and machine scheduling and acquisition. Even though the overall hours for the month may be sufficient to achieve the schedule, if there is an overload in one week and an underload in the next week, timeliness of orders can be affected. If the overloaded area is a feeder area for another internal resource, the expected work may not arrive at the downstream work center on schedule. This can have a ripple effect on the downstream work area. Even though the capacity was planned and available, if the expected work does not arrive, shipments will not be completed as expected. Effective bill of resource use allows the detailed planning for these resources so that all schedules can be met on time.

## Production Control

The production control function releases paperwork and job orders at every level of the bill of material. One assumption of MRP is that all materials go into and out of stock. Selecting from the options of either bill of material levels or routing steps as the best way to identify the product can be a complex task. Many factors must be considered to make the best solution. Unlike some decisions, there is not one correct answer. Both tools have their best application. Using a flat head screwdriver to turn a Phillips head screw is possible, but the result usually is stripping the head of the screw, bending the screwdriver, and becoming frustrated. The best solution is to use a correctly sized Phillips head screwdriver for the Phillips head screw. The same thing happens for bills of material and routings. Overstructuring the bill of material by having too many levels leads to excess work in production control as employees open, close, and track orders at every level in the bill. Not having enough levels in the bill of material can adversely affect the controls within the company. More levels in the bill of material allow costing at a finer level of detail. This finer level of detail comes at a cost with the increased paperwork and transaction volume. The quantity of levels of the bill is dependent on how the product will be put together. The rule of thumb is that if the item will be tracked, stored, or sold in that state of processing, a level in the bill of material is required. If the state of processing is temporary, then a routing step is more appropriate.

The engineering drawing may define more levels than are used in the actual manufacture of the product. Manufacturing has no desire to track, store, or sell the part in that configuration, but engineering has developed a drawing for it. Compromise can be reached by using an item called phantom or "blow through" part numbers. Phantom numbers have no lead time and are not expected to have any inventory. APICS in the 8th edition dictionary defines the phantom bill of material as

> A bill of material coding and structuring technique used primarily for transient (nonstocked) subassemblies. For the transient item, lead time is set to zero and the order quantity to lot for lot. A phantom bill of material represents an item that is physically built, but rarely stocked, before being used in the next step or level of manufacturing. This permits MRP logic to drive requirements straight through the phantom item to its components, but the MRP system usually retains its ability to net against any occasional inventories of the item. This technique also facilitates the use of common bills of material for engineering and manufacturing.

Other names for this concept include pseudo bill of material, make on assembly (MOA), and transient bill of material. The phantom part is an excellent way to ensure that the bills of material used in the company are identical for all functions and that each gets the visibility it requires. Some computer systems allow the identification of different item types within the bill of material. Views of the bills of material are available based on these view types. The most important thing to remember is that one, and only one, bill of material should exist in the company.

## Marketing

Another use for phantom items is for marketing. Phantom items can be used to identify drawing numbers or other groupings of product for planning purposes. The concept of a phantom bill of material can be used by the marketing function when forecasting sales for product groups. Projected sales for the product group are expected to break down into known ratios for each parent item in the product group. Marketing also uses these phantom bills of material to identify product groups for niche identification and sales strategy development. The product group is not really built, but data can be collected and forecasts can be developed for this high-level group. Remember that forecasts for larger accumulations of parts are more accurate. For the make-to-order company, this application can plan long lead time critical resources required for the company, such as engineering time, overall direct labor time, and cash availability as a direct relationship to the level of sales for a product group. The phantom product groups are really never built, but the summary information can be critical to running the company. This long-term visibility allows the top management team to calculate the resource requirements rather than forecasting them with all the inherent inaccuracy. The resulting accuracy has far-reaching impact. Just like having MRP plan materials, planning critical resources proactively allows planning sufficient resources at the right place, at the right time. The net result is a more competitive company.

## BUILDING THE BILL OF MATERIAL

Bills of material are structured starting at the top-level parent item. All parts required to make this final end item are on the first level of the bill of material. Bills of material levels are numbered starting with zero for the parent item. The levels are counted, in increasing steps of one, moving through the structure to the purchased materials. This is the reverse of intuition, where it would be logical to start at the bottom and count up. Every MRP system uses the convention of starting with zero at the top and counting down through the bill of material levels. The bill of material depth is considered the largest number counted. For example, the bill of material in Table 4–1 is two levels deep.

**T A B L E   4–1**

Multilevel Bill of Material

| Parent Item ID 89547, Sportsman's Special Rod | | | | |
|---|---|---|---|---|
| Level | Item ID | Item Name | Qty per Assy | Unit of Measure |
| 0 | 89547 | Sportsman's special rod | | Each |
| .1 | 14358 | Guides, black | 5 | Each |
| .1 | 34926 | Blank, rod, graphite, 2 sections | 1 | Each |
| .2 | 43086 | Graphite, prepreg. | 6 | Lin. Yd. |
| .1 | 89326 | Grip, cork | 1 | Each |

The graphite prepreg (43086) goes into only the rod blank (34926). In turn, the rod blank (34926) goes into the finished goods Sportsman's rod (89547). This would be a two-level deep bill of material. The purchased parts in this bill of material are the black guides (14358), the graphite prepreg (43086), and the cork grips (89326). These items have no additional items structured beneath them; therefore, they must be purchased.

The bill of material is stored in the computer as a series of single-level bills. If only a partial display is made of a bill of material, the level identifier may look as if it changes. The level identifier tracks what goes into what. Bills of material are entered into the computer system in a single-level format. The software will link the appropriate bills together because of the unique identifier used. Figures 4–1 and 4–2 show two single-level bills of material that are the subcomponents of the fully indented bill of material in Table 4–1.

The indented relationship of the finished rod to the rod blank and ultimately to the purchased raw material is built up through this series of single-level bill of material entries.

A rule of thumb is that the MRP system will process requirements more quickly given shallower (fewer levels) bills of material. Most companies can fully structure their product in less than five levels. More than five levels signifies a long product processing time due to many intermediate subassemblies that are completed and stored. Work orders at each level must be created, issued, and received. More levels in the bills of material signify

**FIGURE 4–1**

Bill of Material Listing

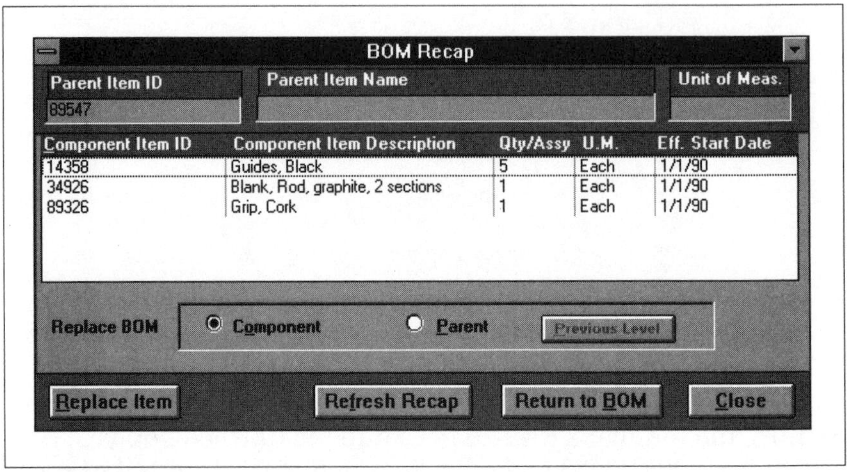


**FIGURE 4–2**

Single-Item Bill of Material

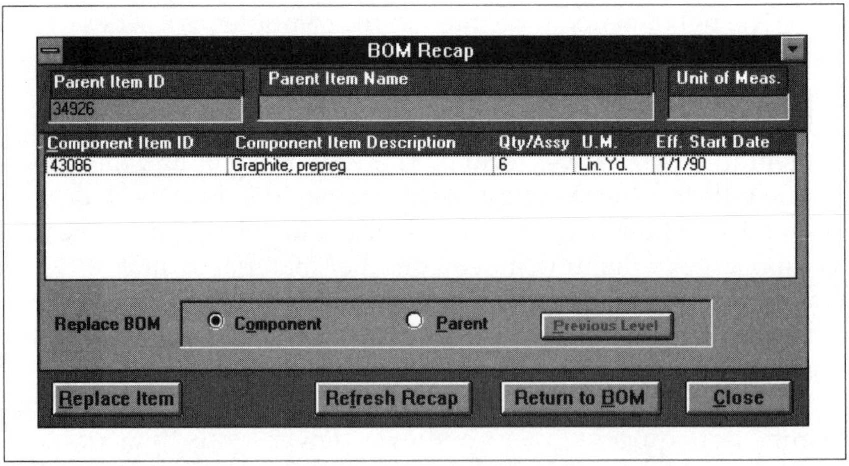


more paperwork in the factory and longer lead times. Fewer bill of material levels usually signifies a faster, simpler product processing time. The item in the last position of the bill of material must be a purchased part. If the last item in line is not purchased, the bills of material have not been fully structured and component items are missing. If the purchased items are not on the bill of material, complete planning visibility will not be possible.

Usually the reason why the lowest-level items are not purchased parts is disagreement on the unit of measure for the item, so the item is omitted from the bill. Some components are purchased by the pound, stocked by the sheet, and issued by the square inch. These changing units of measure increase the complexity of the bills of material, as the different functional areas that use them attempt to make them fit their area. Engineering thinks in terms of square inches of metal as the net requirement to build the parts. The stockroom counts the same parts in terms of sheets. The purchasing department buys the material in pounds. So, what to do? Many companies decide just to forecast the materials requirements rather than put them on the bill of material. Since these items are not identified in the bill of material, the material is sometimes not purchased in time to support production. Considering the inherent inaccuracy of forecasting, especially way into the future and in such detail, this is a no-win situation. Purchasing will always have the wrong parts in the wrong quantity on order. Managing these items can make bill of material structuring a challenge. Thankfully, most computer systems have a conversion factor so that purchasing can buy in one unit of measure and the stores function can issue in a different unit of measure. If push comes to shove and no conversion factor is available, the safest bet is to structure the bills of material in units of measure that will be used by the shop floor. The floor transactions outnumber any other transactions in the system. Helping these transactions be more accurate will enhance the overall accuracy of the system. The bill of material should reflect how the product is really built.

## BILLS OF RESOURCE

Bills of resource are really the same as bills of material except the items on the bill are consumable resources that cannot be stored and inventoried. Try as hard as we might, capacity from yesterday cannot be stored in the stockroom and used tomorrow. This inability to stock consumable resources makes the overall planning process for resources critical. Inventory can be used to buffer errors in planning. Unfortunately, resources cannot be inventoried. The goal is to have sufficient resources at the right place, at the right time, without any waste. Excess consumable resources cannot be carried over to the next period as can inventory. Workers who are idle on Monday are not able to double output on Tuesday.

Insufficient resources will cause schedules to be missed and will likely affect the customer negatively. These customers can be internal or external. An overload at one work center can adversely affect work at later work centers as expected work does not arrive to consume the downstream work center's resource. Typical resources tracked on a bill of resources include labor-hours, machine-hours, square footage, and cash. The question to ask is, What do we need to add to get more output? Sometimes the answer can be surprising. Machine-hours could be tracked in detail, but if there are more machines than people, the information really required may be labor-hours. Frustration reigns when the information is needed in labor-hours and the answers keep coming back in machine-hours. Resources must be identified that are constraints to the process output. The computerized MRP system is not an intelligent being. MRP will not translate what you said to what you mean. MRP simply summarizes and crunches the data you feed it.

At the Production Plan level, the planned resources are long lead items, including specialized machines and total direct labor requirements. As the planning becomes more detailed in the master production schedule, resource planning changes and becomes more detailed in the rough-cut capacity plan. Shorter lead time resources are planned, including assembly labor, fabrication labor, and bottleneck machine time. At the most detailed level, using the output from MRP, bills of resource can plan the capacity required at each specific work area through a process called capacity requirements planning. The important thing to note is that all resource planning is driven by the priority plan. Unlike the Production Plan being further detailed into the master production schedule, and the master production schedule adding together into the Production Plan, the resource plan can and should be very different for each level. Critical resources change as the planning horizon changes. In addition, resources planned can change over time as the demands on the business and the market change. A piece of equipment that is critical this year may have excess capacity next year as the production mix changes. The closèd-loop approach to planning is essential to keep abreast of the changes required as the competitive arena shifts.

## CONFIGURATION CONTROL

Bills of material control the final product configuration. Traceability documentation of the final part configuration is important to some businesses for product liability concerns. For other companies, the "as built" traceability is not critical. In most businesses, documentation of the "as built" product can be used if there is ever a need for a spare part or replacement of a subassembly. Validating that the "as designed" definition agrees with the "as built" configuration is important in controlling configuration and serviceability of the parent item.

Configuration change control is the process of managing the evolution of the bill of material. Changes can be made because of engineering improvements, customer change requests, material substitutions, or any other reason that requires changes to the bill of material. Date effectivity is one way to control the changes to the bill of material. One part is used until a prespecified date, and then another part or series of parts is substituted. Predicting the date when the part is expected to cut over can cause some problems since it tends to follow the same rules of forecasting— always wrong and worse further into the future.

In response to this problem, another method of configuration control, serial number effectivity, can be used. This process defines the parts to be used on sequentially numbered units that are tracked by serial number no matter what the due date. The difficulty here is predicting how much of the component will be used on each parent item until the cut-over serial number. If there is any variability in material utilization, this forecasting can be as bad as date effectivity. The process does not work at all if serial numbers are not used. Finding computer software that will track configuration control by serial number is more difficult and usually more expensive. The more common solution is the date effectivity process.

## Making Configuration Changes

MRP will look ahead and plan the existing part for all demand prior to the change date, then plan the replacement item after that. When determining on what date to make a change, the current available inventory must be considered. Making a change could potentially leave some inventory without any demands: obsolete inventory. Part of making an effective configuration change is to determine how many dollars of obsolete inventory may result. Having all functional areas use the same bill of material allows this analysis to take place in a fairly easy manner. A method to ensure that all the old inventory will be used up before the new part is requested is to structure the new part as a component of the old part, using the phantom logic described earlier for the out-going part. The old part's lead time is set to zero, and the order method is identified as lot for lot. MRP will then use all the old parts before planning any requirements for the new part. This procedure is effective when the following conditions are all true:

- Demand rate is not known. An estimate at a cut-over date or serial number effectivity is not possible.

- There is a one-to-one part change. A phantom can be used to connect one part to another but is not effective attempting to connect many to one or one to many. This process can become very complex and confusing very fast.

- The desire is to use all the old material. This procedure will consume all the material before planning the parts change. If there is a strategic reason to make the change sooner, this may not be feasible.

- Coordinated cost roll-ups occur. After the cut-over has occurred, the bill of material must be changed, removing the old parts and keeping the new parts, to maintain bill of material accuracy. Confusion may occur if the financial department performs a cost roll-up before these changes are made to the bill of material. The costs of the new part and all its components are counted along with the costs of the old part and all its components. This weakness is only a problem if standard costs are rerolled on a frequent basis. For most companies this process is done on an annual basis, and the bill of material has been previously updated to remove the old parts. Any unusual changes in standard costs will be noted in the standard cost process roll-up before the final changes are made.

The most difficult part of this process is remembering to go back and remove the temporary phantom structure. This requires that records are kept of any pending bill of material change. In small companies, this usually does not prove too difficult, and the process ensures that the old material is totally consumed. This method will not work if a series of parts needs to change at the same time in one coordinated change. The better method for this kind of change is to determine a most-likely effective date and continue to monitor inventory until the change. The time spent monitoring this type of change will depend on the value of the inventory and whether it can be used somewhere else. The higher the possible cost of obsolete inventory, the more time can be spent monitoring the change. If the benefits do not exceed the cost, don't do it!

Sometimes the bill of material requires immediate change either to correct an error or a safety issue or in direct response to the customer. The date effectivity process works well to accommodate this type of change. The date is changed to the current date, and MRP will provide visibility to the material planner of the immediate nature of the need for the new material when the work orders are planned. Even though this material may have a past-due requirement date, at least the planner knows about the need and the priority, can peg them to where the demands originated, and develop realistic production schedules to address the situation. Once again, having a single company bill of material is essential for effective communication of the potential impact of this type of change.

## Planning Bills of Material

### Superbills (S Bills)
Bills of material can be developed for groups of things that are never really built. These planning bills can improve the overall effectiveness of the planning function. The master scheduler can use product groups to define planning bills of material to

streamline the entry of the master schedule. These bills of material are known as superbills, or S bills. They are phantom-type bills of material that collect together various product modules for planning. The advantage of superbills is that even though the top-end item is never really built, the grouping is logical and matches how the products are thought of within the organization for facilities forecasting and master scheduling. Many times the proportions of sales for each product stay about the same, but the overall sales volume can change. The superbill allows the projected dollars from the business plan or Production Plan to be entered and then translated into units required. This grouping of products increases the accuracy of the forecasting efforts and makes the master scheduling process easier. The use of superbills is dependent on the type of business involved. Some product groups for a fishing rod manufacturing company could be:

PG1 Commercial Product
   SG 1 Bass rods
   SG 2 Salmon rods
   SG 3 Steelhead rods
PG2 OEM Product
   SG 4 Retail
   SG 5 Private label

Each of these product groups can then be broken into specific buildable part numbers.

SG1 Bass Rods
   85259 Super Bass Rod (2 each)
   25377 Deluxe Bass Rod (10 each)
   12054 Super Deluxe Bass Rod (20 each)

Quantities can then be defined for the distribution of sales within these product groups. For example, for every unit of SG1 sold (a unit could be $1K), there are 2 each 85259, 10 each 25377, and 20 each 12054. This can be represented in a superbill and used for planning purposes. One company reduced its master production schedule entry time from three days for two people to two hours for one person through the use of superbills. Instead of planning thousands of numbers, the master scheduler only had to enter a schedule for 100 product groups. Forecasting and planning is more accurate at this high level of aggregation. A small company that makes fan blades for trucks and cars uses superbills for both forecasting and master scheduling. In both cases, the overall accuracy and timeliness of the master schedule improved by using this new tool.

### Kit Bills (K Bills)

Another method of structuring bills of material is the use of the kit bill, or K bill. If the end item contains many small parts that may be shipped loose, or the same group of fasteners are used on many different units, it may be a good idea to group all these under a kit number. The kit number is added to the next higher level of the bill of material. The advantage is that even though the sack of parts may never be assembled into a finished unit, having only one number represent a set of parts simplifies the overall maintenance and accuracy of the bills of material. A standard kit can be added to many different end products. This is simpler and more accurate. Having a K bill provides the option of shipping a separate kit of parts with the main assembly. In this case the K bill parent would have a standard type item identifier. In other cases, the item structure of the kit bill is a phantom structure only used to group parts. This still allows the company to build the kits to stock during slack periods, easing the parts issuing process during busy periods if the business is seasonal. The K bill can be an important tool for a company with the need to manage large groups of small parts.

### Pegging

Standard bills of material, superbills, phantom bills, and kit bills all describe the ingredients needed to make a product. The real power of a bill of material is not just the ability to view the structure top down but also bottom up. Bills of material not only communicate what component is used to make a parent item, they also communicate information in the other direction. Where is a component used? This pegging, or implosion function, is very valuable to the material or capacity planner. When difficulty arises with a specific component part or when an engineering change is pending on a part, the planner wants to know immediately where the part is used and how many end items and customers will be affected. The pegging process links the parts upwards to the parent part. Options exist to peg only one level or to peg all the way up to the end item. Table 4–2 is an example of a single-level where-used report. The graphite prepreg used in the rod blank (34926) introduced earlier in the chapter is also used on a three-piece rod blank (32856). If something happened to the supply of prepreg, the impact to potential production can be seen immediately.

When all the parents of components are required, the answer is the multilevel where used. This report shows all the relationships of the component selected to all higher-level related parents in increasing order of relationship. Table 4–3 is an example of a multilevel where-used report. Since there is no parent for the rod blank number 35870, the assumption can be made that this is an end-item part for shipment to the customer.

## Accuracy

Accuracy is essential for every bill of material since this document is used throughout the company. The two most important inputs to MRP are the unique identification of a part and an accurate bill of material. These two inputs drive everything else MRP does. The effects of an inaccurate bill of material reach all areas of the organization. Purchasing could order the incorrect parts or in the incorrect quantities. Manufacturing could build the wrong parts.

TABLE  4–2

Where Used—Single Level

| Component Item ID | Component Name | Unit of Measure |
|---|---|---|
| 43086 | Graphite, prepreg | Lin. Yd. |
| **Parent Item ID** | **Parent Description** | **Quantity per Assembly** |
| 34926 | Blank, rod, graphite, 2 sections | 6.00 |
| 32856 | Blank, rod, graphite, 3 sections | 5.00 |

Parts might not fit together since the wrong parts were issued to the floor. Finance would incorrectly cost a product, resulting in subsequent poor management decisions. Many other adverse results can be linked to the incorrect bill of material. Soon the process has deteriorated into every department keeping records on its own—a sure sign of trouble! The informal system is always waiting for this kind of trouble, and remember where that gets you.

A practical approach to verifying the bills of material—"as designed," "as built," "as documented"—is to send a copy of the engineering bill of material to the shop floor for validation as the product is being built. This closes the feedback loop between "as designed" and "as built." The important issue using this method is that for any discrepancy found, the correction must be made in a timely fashion. Otherwise, the production department will quickly realize that this is an exercise in futility and will not spend its scarce resources doing this activity. If the updates and corrections are made quickly, benefits can be seen immediately.

Another way to validate the bill of material is to take a product from inventory, tear it down, and match the resulting components with the current bill of material. Sometimes this process yields many surprises for product designers when they discover what actually goes into a part they designed. Which process is

**TABLE  4–3**

Where Used—Multilevel

| Where Used: | Component Item ID | Component Name | |
|---|---|---|---|
| | 43086 | Graphite, prepreg | |
| **Item ID** | **Item Name** | **Unit Of Measure** | **Qty/Assy** |
| 43086 | Graphite, prepreg | Lin. Yd. | 6.00 |
| 34926 | Blank, rod, graphite, 2 sections | Each | 1.00 |
| 89547 | Sportsman's special rod | Each | 1.00 |
| 43086 | Graphite, prepreg | Lin. Yd. | 5.00 |
| 35870 | Blank, rod, graphite, 3 sections | Each | 4.00 |

chosen depends on the product at hand and how it is put together. Some finished goods are impossible to tear apart once they have been assembled. In this case, the validation sheet traveling with the work order would be the best choice of tools. No matter the method chosen, validating bills of material is required to ensure accuracy. Accuracy is critical for an effective MRP system.

Accuracy in the bills of material is required to be at least 98 percent for an MRP system to be successful. Accuracy is calculated by determining the number of bill of material lines that have no error. This is then divided by the total number of lines checked. The result is expressed as a percentage. When the bill of material calls for 100 parts and only 90 are found in the assembly, this does not mean that the bill of material is 90 percent accurate. Each line is evaluated and compared to the engineering drawing to determine accuracy. If 20 lines of 25 lines are correct, then the bill of material is 80 percent accurate. When cumulative accuracy is considered, this would be a very bad situation. If this bill of material is 80 percent accurate and the next bill of material is 80 percent accurate, the chances that the right parts will be ordered and available for both products is only 72 percent. The key is not just whether the MRP system matches the engineering drawing, but that the product matches the designer's intent and the final customer's needs.

## BILL OF MATERIAL CHALLENGES

Different parts can cause challenges when structuring a bill of material. Some of the most difficult parts are fasteners and other small, very low-cost parts that are used on virtually every product. Many companies do not control fasteners by issuing them to the job. Other companies track down to every nut, bolt, and fastener. Ideally, everything used to build the product should be on the bill of material to provide visibility of future requirements and develop complete costs. However, the reality is that a choice is sometimes made not to spend the time and expense of putting these items on the bill. The cost of this detailed tracking exceeds the cost of the material being tracked. The decision could be made to keep "large" stocks of them available for use when needed.

The problem is that, if the product mix changes drastically, different fasteners can be required. A missing washer costing a fraction of a cent can prevent the shipment of a very expensive product. The little things become very big things when they are needed and are not available. A good middle ground is to put the fasteners on the bill of material for planning purposes but bulk issue the parts to the manufacturing line. These small items could be expensed at the time they are issued. If the fasteners are a significant cost component, backflushing can be used to move the costs of the fasteners onto the parent item's production. The choice of tools is made by analyzing the cost and benefit of these different levels of control. This allows the forward planning strength of MRP to ensure that the right parts are available at the right time while minimizing inventory without spending more money than it's worth tracking fasteners to each job.

Another difficulty in structuring bills of material is dealing with items that do not vary with the quantity of product being built. A good example is two-part epoxy. Once the epoxy is mixed, one part or 100 parts may be built using virtually the same amount of material. These items are shown on the bill of material as a quantity of "per order." MRP then knows that each order only requires one of this component for each order rather than multiplying the quantity by the order size. If these "per order" items have significant cost, the number of parts that can be built from one unit may drive the manufacturing lot size.

## SUMMARY

Accurate bills of material and bills of resources are essential for a closed-loop MRP system. The MRP system uses these relationships to calculate what is required, how much, and when. The planner can make proactive plans to accommodate upcoming material issues and known capacity imbalances. Even without an automated closed-loop MRP system, the manufacturing department must know what goes into building the end item. This is a basic requirement for any manufacturing business. Many different tools are available for planning and using bills of material. The application and underlying requirements must be well understood to select the right tool for the job. Using the proper tools to manage this key company document directly impacts the overall success of the business.

# 5

## INVENTORY RECORD ACCURACY

### INTRODUCTION

Material Requirements Planning (MRP) is an excellent planning tool. MRP aligns material availability with material requirements. Any time material requirements and replenishments are not aligned, messages are sent to the planner concerning the mismatch. No longer do the material planners have to examine and consider every part number at planning time. Planning is done by exception. A single planner can effectively manage more parts than ever before. Using the master production schedule and the bills of materials, MRP calculates the requirements for future materials. This future visibility allows the planner to make intelligent decisions concerning the detailed scheduling and management of the shop. Knowing an accurate projected demand for a part allows the planner to take advantage of combining setups and increasing overall manufacturing efficiency. Rather than being in the position of fire fighting, the planner has a realistic view of the business's future and the manufacturing requirements required to support that plan. The planner can plan strategically and help the company achieve its desired goals and objectives.

Decisions concerning lot sizes and frequency of runs can be tied to overall business objectives concerning inventory levels and customer service. The business process flow must be well understood, however, before these tools can be fit to controlling the process. Just as the manufacturing process and machines have controls, the data in the Material Requirements Planning system must be controlled. Critical data elements are the bills of material and inventory record accuracy. Bill of material accuracy was covered in Chapter 4. Inventory record accuracy is so dynamically affected by everything in the system and process that it demands a chapter of its own.

MRP takes the master schedule and explodes it through the bills of material to determine what the gross requirements are for component parts. For example, if the plant was assembling bicycles, the bill of material would call out two wheels for every bike. If the plan was to build 100 bikes, the gross requirement for wheels would be 200. The dependent demand for wheels does not have to be a guess or forecast. The demand can be calculated exactly from the master production schedule. The gross requirement is then compared to the available quantity to determine what additional parts, if any, must be procured or made to support the overall schedule. Since it is unlikely that the inventory of wheels will exactly match the overall needs from the master production schedule, an order is placed to purchase or make any required wheels.

For many reasons, the lot size for building or purchasing wheels can be very different from the lot size for building bikes. Overall business management issues will drive the quantity of inventory desired to service the demand for the bikes. Any error in the bills of material or inventory on-hand balances will result in incorrect action notices being sent to the planner. Even worse than bad planner information is the impact on the organization of having excess inventory or a shortage of critical parts. Every MRP system on the market today performs the gross-to-net requirement accurately. Isn't it interesting how we blame the computer when the information that comes out is incorrect? Keep in mind the adage about computers—GIGO—garbage in, garbage out. To ensure that garbage is not being fed to the computer, the critical pieces of data used for calculations must be verified.

## INVENTORY RECORD ACCURACY

Some methods that can be used to ensure inventory record accuracy are mass balance, annual physical inventory, and cycle counting. Mass balance adds up all the incoming receipts and deducts materials used based on what has shipped to the customer. The resulting mass balance is expected to be found in inventory. This method is used in cases where the inventory is especially difficult to count, such as material stored in silos or rail cars. The reality of this approach is that the resulting actual on-hand balance usually bears little resemblance to the expected quantity on hand. Unexpected events occur that use extra inventory and, if the operation is of any significant size, tracking multiple items in this manner can be very unwieldy. In the face of having no other system, many companies use the mass balance method to value and validate their inventory. The accuracy of each individual part is extremely suspect, and this method cannot be used with an MRP system. One of the requirements of MRP is that there are inventory records for all parts.

The most commonly used and the second less preferable method is the annual physical inventory. This process closes the entire facility for the duration of the counting and uses everyone in the plant to count unfamiliar parts. The worst inventory write-down in one company's history was directly attributable to the annual physical inventory. One of the counters was unfamiliar with the parts and proceeded to count some electrostatic discharge sensitive parts (translation: very expensive and damaged easily) by stripping them from their protective sleeves and weigh-counting them. This parts handling process caused many of the parts to be scrapped and thousands of dollars of inventory writeoff for the company. Further problems were caused because the assembly department was now short these critical parts and expedited replacements had to be air shipped from the supplier.

To perform an effective physical inventory, the following steps are required.

• *Ensure that all transactions are completed.* This is essential for an accurate count. All receipt and issue transactions must have the same deadline. After all the transactions are completed, freeze all activity with the inventory. Receipts from suppliers and shipments to the customers must have a clean cutoff point so that the perpetual inventory records can be updated. Many companies send messages to the suppliers and customers communicating the expected dates of the annual physical inventory and that there will be no shipments received or delivered during this inventory time.

• *Control counts through inventory tags.* Each item counted is tagged with a control tag. Part of the tag is left with the item and part is brought back for entry into the computer or validated against the manual records. Leaving a portion of the tag on the item ensures that all items have been counted. Items not expected to be counted are identified with a tag that says "Non-inventory item." This rigid approach to identification of counted and uncounted items and a clean cutoff from shipments and receipts attempts to ensure positive control of every item in the plant. After the inventory has been counted and the tags have been entered into the computer or validated against the manual inventory, required reports are run.

• *Run analysis reports.* These reports summarize the total inventory change in dollars and are usually sorted by the variances against the perpetual inventory record.

• *Recount significant variance items.* If the errors are great, items may need to be recounted. Expect that 80 percent of the dollar problems will be attributed to 20 percent of the errors. After recounting the items with significant variances, the accountants then verify the inventory and clear sections of the plant to continue production. Depending on the size of the plant, this process can be completed in one day or several days.

One thing remains constant—the annual physical inventory always takes longer than expected or desired. The result of this antiquated process of annual physical inventory is an unfounded confidence in the accuracy of the inventory records, since the perpetual record is updated during this time.

Most personnel involved in the annual physical inventory have one goal: to complete the task quickly. The accuracy of the inventory is of secondary importance to them. Taking the physical inventory is repetitive, dirty work that few people enjoy. Even the accountants care only about the total dollar impact to the balance sheet. This is why a reserve is created on the balance sheet to accommodate the potential of an inventory write-down (losing dollars of inventory). The inventory shrink is a budgeted line item in many businesses. Provided that the annual physical results in a loss less than expected, the accountants are happy. Accountants are responsible for managing dollars, not parts.

The classic story of 100 percent inventory record accuracy is that a bank at the end of each day must account for all of its inventory. A teller in a bank is much like a storekeeper recording all the inventory receipts and issues. Each day tellers are expected to account for the overall inventory under their control. Having pieces of their inventory disappear is not treated with the same apathy as losing inventory in a manufacturing operation. The expectation is that tellers will account for every last dollar and cent. While the overall accuracy of banks is impressive and their positive controls and tracking documents provide them excellent visibility of the day's business, they enjoy the benefit of having interchangeable inventory. If there is an overage on $20 bills, as long as there is an offsetting shortage of $10 or $5 bills and the total dollars add up, the teller is satisfied with the overall accuracy.

In a manufacturing plant, the reality is that forgings cannot be easily substituted for integrated circuits even when their value may be the same. Even more difficult is the medical device or aerospace industries, where traceability of lots is required. Having the correct number of a certain part is not sufficient. The number of parts by each lot number must agree with the overall inventory system. Some companies even count by part, by lot number, and by location to assess overall inventory accuracy. Even if only one factor is off, they consider it an inaccurate inventory record.

World-class organizations rarely voluntarily disrupt their entire inventory and operation by imposing an annual physical inventory. The commonly held belief that auditors require an annual physical inventory is not true. Not one of the Big 6 accounting firms requires an annual physical inventory. The process of validating the asset called inventory is required, but an annual physical inventory is not. Keeping well-organized, accurate perpetual inventory records benefits the operation more than just eliminating the physical inventory. The daily output of the MRP system and the real-time analysis of the financials through the MRPII closed-loop function is possible with a high level of assurance. The annual physical inventory is a carryover from a time when we did not have the systems or disciplines to maintain an accurate perpetual inventory. Cycle counting is an alternative method to validating the inventory asset and provides better operating results.

## CYCLE COUNTING

Cycle counting is the preferred method of validating the inventory process. This allows small quantities of the inventory to be counted daily or weekly by personnel that know and understand the parts. The real benefit of cycle counting is not the update of the physical inventory records but rather the identification and resolution of the root causes of inventory record inaccuracy. There is less time between the cause and the detection of errors. Try to remember what you had for dinner last night. That can be hard enough. Attempting to remember why a transaction was done eight months ago is virtually impossible. The investment for cycle counting is significantly less than the annual physical inventory. Because a little is done each day, the risk for large inventory losses is greatly reduced. Just eliminating this financial impact and the management shock of the annual writeoff can be sufficient to support a cycle counting program. The people counting the parts are familiar with the parts and their required handling. Since cycle counting is part of their everyday duty, the learning curve effect is seen and they become very efficient and quick at performing the counts. More counts can be accurately completed at a lower cost than the annual physical inventory.

### Cycle Counting Requirements

#### Unique Part Numbers
As in many other parts of the MRP system, each item in inventory must be identifiable through a unique number. This means that if a part is in inventory in a number of different conditions, such as unpainted, painted, and plated, each condition of the part must have a unique part number. If a part has the same part number, the fit, form, and function must be identical. A good test is that if a blind-folded person could reach into the bin and use any part drawn, then that should be one part number. If a sort would have to occur

to have a useable part, then a different part number is required. Unique part numbers are required for MRP to run anyway. This is not a new requirement to support cycle counting. Unique part identification allows error-free communication about parts.

### Experienced Counters

The people performing the counting should have experience in counting and be able to handle numbers accurately. This means that people responsible for maintaining the inventory should be evaluated for their ability to read and write numbers accurately. Even very intelligent people can be challenged when it comes to handling numbers. Each person responsible for counting the inventory should be validated in their counting process so that one uniform process is used throughout the company. Experienced counters have the responsibility and accountability for accurate inventory. High attention to detail is required in this position.

### Control Group

A representative group of parts is selected for testing the overall cycle count and inventory process. This group should contain representatives from each product group and dollar category. The control group is used during the early stages of cycle counting to validate the inventory control process. It is also used from time to time to validate any changes made in the counting process. Establishing a control group is a key factor for success in any cycle counting program. This is usually the overlooked part of the process.

### System for Tracking Inventory

Inventory record accuracy is not dependent on the use of a computer. Many small companies envy the sophisticated computer systems of larger companies. An expensive computer system is not a requirement for accurate inventory; positive controls are. Any reliable system for tracking inventory movement both in and out and the resulting perpetual balance are adequate for the cycle counting process. Not uncommon in small businesses is tracking inventory on a manual card or simple spreadsheet. Provided the system is reliable and updated in a timely fashion, the resulting information should be accurate. The focus must be on the process and not on the tool used. Manual systems can be more accurate than automated ones. Automating a bad manual process will still give bad information—just faster.

**Small Amount of Time Each Day for Counting**
The best time for counting is when all transactions have been posted against the database or manual record. Counting first thing in the morning is the most common process used. The amount of time dedicated to counting and validating those counts should not exceed 30 to 60 minutes. The main thrust of cycle counting is to accomplish a small bit each day and not impact the overall operation. This dedicated small amount of time each day yields major benefits for the operation. The discipline required to dedicate this time each day can become a challenge as the company becomes busier and the time demands of the storekeepers increase. Discipline is necessary to maintain accurate inventories and allocating time to count is only a small part of the total requirement, but it is essential for the process to be successful.

## CYCLE COUNTING—1,2,3

Many different approaches are used to accomplish cycle counting. A proven method is the seven-step approach that follows.

### Step 1: Identify ABC Groups

The most popular way to identify ABC groups is to rank inventory by dollars used. Options are to use the projected usage based on MRP output or to use historical usage. The usage is multiplied by the value of the part. These dollarized values are then sorted from low to high, and a natural break will occur between the "A" items and "B" items. "A" items are those 15 to 20 percent of the items that account for 80 percent of the total value. The "B" items follow with approximately another 30 to 50 percent of the items accounting for 10 to 15 percent of the remaining value. The "insignificant many" item numbers left are the "C" items. These are 50 to 60 percent of the number of item numbers but only account for 10 to 15 percent of the total value. Most computerized systems will automatically calculate the ABC groups based on the previously described method.

Another method for identifying ABC class is to rank parts based on lead time for replenishment. Those 20 percent of the parts with the longest lead times will be classified as "A" items. Items readily available will be classified as "C" items. Intermediate items are considered "B" items. This method addresses the strategic nature of the parts and how long it takes to recover them if an unexpected problem arises. Even though a part may not be used in many places and may be low in value, a crisis can develop if an unexpected demand or shortage occurs and the part is a long lead time item. Conversely, it is easier to recover when a part is readily available. Both methods can be utilized by a knowledgeable planner who understands the overall process and the significance of a particular part. The planner can upgrade a part to a higher class or move a part to a lower class. A wise discipline is that, for every item promoted from B to A, another item should be demoted from A to B. Otherwise, the number of A items can grow to become larger than is appropriate. Table 5–1 shows a sample A, B, C listing by value.

## Step 2: Select a Control Group

The control group should be a small cross-section of all the parts under perpetual inventory control. This control group will be used to validate the inventory control process. The group should be no more than can be counted in 30 minutes. For the average small company this is 10 to 15 different part numbers. The control group should include items that move quickly and slowly, high- and low-dollar items, large and small parts. Each type of manufacturing inventory—components, semifinished goods, and finished goods—should be included in the group. Unfortunately and incorrectly, this step is skipped by many companies starting the cycle count process. The control group provides a very valuable function by clearly identifying process issues.

## Step 3: Count the Control Group Repeatedly

Many companies attempt to pass over this step, but it is the most critical for long-term success. The control group items should be counted daily until 100 percent inventory accuracy is achieved

**TABLE  5–1**

Sample ABC Report

| Item ID | Item Name | Usage Value | Class Code |
|---------|-----------|-------------|------------|
| 89547 | Sportsman's special rod | $2,221.35 | A |
| 25377 | Bass rod | $2,212.40 | A |
| 85259 | Freshwater fisher | $1,775.67 | A |
| 34926 | Blank, rod, graphite, 2 sections | $1,726.47 | A |
| 12054 | Custom configuration rod | $1,537.96 | A |
| 43086 | Graphite, prepreg | $1,347.53 | A |
| 98005 | Belt guard, 3x4 ball mill | $ 609.59 | B |
| 93874 | Blank, rod, graphite, 2 sections | $ 247.89 | B |
| 35870 | Blank, rod, glass, 2 sections | $ 237.40 | B |
| 32856 | Blank, rod, graphite, 3 sections | $ 123.13 | B |
| 98015 | Head top plate, LV-60/80 H mill | $ 33.90 | B |
| 74070 | Grip, A/W cork | $ 17.55 | B |
| 45877 | Reel seat, silver/gold | $ 13.95 | B |
| 90432 | Grip, foam black | $ 9.95 | C |
| 84567 | Grips, cork | $ 8.95 | C |
| 89326 | Grip, cork | $ 8.95 | C |
| 90247 | Reel seat, frosted silver | $ 7.95 | C |
| 14358 | Guides, black | $ 6.70 | C |
| 74988 | Reel seat, gold/black | $ 6.49 | C |
| 57420 | Reel seat, black | $ 5.89 | C |
| 64123 | Guides, stainless | $ 5.35 | C |
| 23049 | Epoxy, 2 part | $ 5.35 | C |
| 34589 | O-ring, 1/4", rubber, hardened, new, quoted | $ 5.00 | C |
| 23445 | O-ring, 1/4", rubber, hardened, new, quoted | $ 5.00 | C |
| 84569 | Guides, ceramic | $ 4.85 | C |
| 82476 | Reel seat, steel/black | $ 4.65 | C |
| 98456 | Guides, tops | $ 3.27 | C |
| 90437 | Grip, foam | $ 2.00 | C |

and maintained for 10 days. Any error in the counts is documented, and the underlying systems and inventory control
processes must be improved. The process of recounting a
control group gives intensive attention to a small group and

identifies issues that are likely problems for the balance of the parts. By identifying and fixing problems for this group, the balance of the inventory should be similarly affected in a positive way.

## Step 4: Identify Process Issues

Process issues are any event or cause that results in less than 100 percent inventory accuracy. Common errors are failure to make timely transactions, transposing a number, or undocumented usage of a part. These process issues are easiest to see during the control group counting because the time difference between error cause and effect is very short. Additional process issues will likely be uncovered after the cycle counting practice has expanded to the remainder of the item records.

## Step 5: Correct Process Issues

For any process issue resulting in inventory inaccuracy, the root cause must be determined and resolved. This may include updating the inventory control process, training storekeeping and production personnel in the correct procedure, or insisting on discipline in the inventory control process. Just as a bank will not allow anyone to come in and take what they want without a transaction, manufacturing inventory must be accounted for in a reliable fashion. With the advent of ATM machines, no longer is the teller required to document the transaction at the bank. Similarly, since a storekeeper is not required to document inventory movement, discipline of transactions is required. More companies are moving to having parts stored directly on the production line. This increased availability does not eliminate the need for discipline. Actually, on-line stores increase the amount of discipline required.

## Step 6: Expand to Other Part Numbers

After the inventory control process has been proven reliable with the control group and the inventory accuracy for this group has remained at 100 percent for a period of time (5 to 10 days), expand the cycle count process to the rest of the parts. The increase in inventory accuracy will take an initial jump and then gradually move up from there. The goal of the company is to have 100 percent inventory accuracy. Any inventory inaccuracy causes distrust of the system output in general.

## Step 7: Continue to Resolve Process Issues

As problems arise, resulting in inaccurate perpetual inventory records, the process issues must continue to be identified and resolved. According to Deming, 94 precent of the problems arise from the process itself, and only 6 percent come from people. Don't be too quick to blame an operator for the error when usually there is an underlying process issue. Having simple tools enhances inventory accuracy dramatically. The inventory process must be simple enough so that it is easier to do it correctly than circumvent the system. The simple solution is always the hardest to achieve. Also, remember that the less inventory there is in the plant, the easier it is to count.

## SELECTING PARTS TO COUNT

Now that a process has been defined for cycle counting, and the control group has maintained 100 percent accuracy for at least one consecutive week, how do the counts take place and on what cycle? A few different philosophies exist for selecting the cycle.

## Calendar Frequency Using ABC Classification

The classic definition for cycle counting is to count parts based on a combination of the calendar and their ABC code. "A" items would be counted the most frequently—for example, once per month. "B" items would be counted less frequently, such as once per quarter. "C" items may cycle once per year. One way to calculate the frequency of counting is to examine how many counts that would require each day. For example:

> Assume a 5,000 part item master and 250 work days/year.
> We would expect 1,000 "A" items, 1,500 "B" items, and 2,500 "C" items.

"A" items counted monthly: 12,000 counts per year
"B" items counted quarterly: 6,000 counts per year
"C" items counted annually: 2,500 counts per year
Total counts per year: 20,500
Average counts per day: 82

If this counting load per day is too high, then possibly the count frequency can be reduced:

"A" items counted quarterly: 4,000 counts per year
"B" items counted semiannually: 3,000 counts per year
"C" items counted annually: 2,500 counts per year
Total counts per year: 9,500
Average counts per day: 38

The daily workload for counts must be realistic when compared to the resources available. Otherwise, the job will not be done. Better to plan ahead and reduce the frequency than give up on the process altogether.

## Order Time

Another option for counting is when a part is being ordered. Logically the on-hand balance should be low since an order action is imminent. This validation ensures that accurate ordering will take place since the on-hand balance is verified before committing to acquiring more parts. The problem with this approach is that rarely is the quantity of parts hitting their order time consistently. The demand on the storekeepers can fluctuate widely, and the picking process may become a bottleneck in the procurement or manufacturing process. This process is usually used in conjunction with the timed counting process.

## Receipt Time

Verifying inventory at time of receipt takes advantage of the fact that the inventory should be at its absolute lowest point. Unfortunately, although this is very easy to count, it can be compared to locking the barn door after the horse ran away. Finding out that there are excess or missing parts on receipt of an order does not leave much recovery time. This method is best used in addition to other count strategies.

## Negative Inventory

Many modern computer systems allow the inventory to go negative. This does not mean that if a quantity of parts equal to the negative quantity were placed on the shelf, they would immediately disappear into some magical black hole. Having negative inventory means that more parts were issued than the perpetual inventory records had available. Knowing the magnitude of the negative number is very helpful in identifying the underlying root cause. Usually negative inventory is caused by a failure to transact the receipt of an incoming quantity before it is used. Similar to counting when the product is received, this method is best used in conjunction with a regularly scheduled cycle count.

## Counting by Location

A creative and simple way to cycle through the inventory is to count by inventory location. This will uncover parts that have been misplaced and other surprises lurking on the shelves. The process works by obtaining a perpetual inventory listing by inventory location. This assumes that locations are uniquely identified. Identifying specific locations assists in finding the exact location of the part. An easy method for coding locations is the descending significance relationship. If multiple storerooms are used, the first digit could be the location of the storeroom. Alphabetic characters work well and give ample uniqueness with one digit. This also prevents the confusion of part number and inventory locations. The next set of characters is the rack on which the parts are stored. Usually two digits are sufficient. The next digit is the shelf, starting at the bottom with zero or one. Numbering is started at the bottom shelf to allow growth in the vertical direction. Additional specifics can be built in with the location on the shelf. For example, a part stored in B2313 is stored in stockroom B, on rack 23, on the first shelf in the third position. A part in C0501 is in stockroom C, on rack 5, on the bottom shelf in the first position. With very short identifiers, over 200,000 locations can be uniquely identified. Parts are easier to find because the system is very consistent, predictable, and simple.

This declining significance method supports easy production of a report that lists inventory by expected location. Once this report is produced, the storekeeper takes it to the stockroom and begins to validate the inventory. If the parts are easy to count or there is an obvious error, an actual count is performed. If the parts are difficult to count and there is no obvious error, the part is bypassed. For example, at location C2301, there is a quantity of 7 parts of item 12345. The storekeeper validates that part 12345 is indeed expected in location C2301. Since 7 is an easy number to count, the count is validated or the error is noted and reported back to the perpetual system. Moving to location C2302, the bin holding part 12378 should contain 8,794 parts. When looking at the bin, the storekeeper can see that there are a large number of parts. The 8,794 seems reasonable, and counting them would take at least 15 to 20 minutes. Since spending all that time does not add any value, these parts are bypassed. No count is entered for part 12378, and the storekeeper moves to location C2303 where the bin holding part 24536 should have 9,703 parts. Examination reveals that the bin is holding only about 100 parts. The storekeeper makes an exact count and notes the discrepancy for future problem solving. Using this method, storekeepers can verify many more parts than counting every part in every location. Since the purpose of cycle counting is to validate the inventory control process, the ability to collect more data about the accuracy of the inventory and the reason for possible inaccuracy is better than slogging through the tedious counts of parts that look to be correct anyway. The downside of this approach is that it takes a judgment call on the part of the storekeeper.

Some managers do not believe in even letting the storekeepers see the perpetual inventory counts when doing cycle counting. The reality is that the storekeepers are the most motivated to have accurate inventory, and withholding this information will only make their job more difficult. Using proper measurement systems, they will respond with overall process improvements for inventory accuracy rather than spending the time and effort attempting to circumvent the system. Everyone is a winner. Allowing the storekeepers this judgment really puts the control in the correct hands—the process owner who know most about it and is motivated to improve the process.

## DEFINING ACCURACY

Accuracy seems like an easy term to understand. Intuitively either something is right or wrong. However, the APICS definition for accuracy reveals that things are more complicated than first glance might reveal. The APICS definition for accuracy is:

> The degree of freedom from error or the degree of conformity to a standard. Accuracy is different from precision. For example, four significant digit numbers are less precise than six significant digit numbers; however, a properly computed four significant digit number might be more accurate than an improperly computed six significant digit number. (APICS Dictionary, 8th edition)

Inventory accuracy can be thought of in similar terms. Accuracy is similar to tolerance limits of a manufacturing process. When first beginning to measure inventory accuracy, the tolerances begin broad and then continually improve. The tolerances are usually based on the ABC classification. For example, the following tolerances could be used:

**A Items:** +/− 1 percent. If a count for the item is within this tolerance, the count is considered accurate. If 1,000 parts are expected and 1,007 are found in the bin, the count is considered accurate. The actual piece count would be input into the perpetual system, but the count would still be considered accurate. If the tolerance of 1 percent allows high levels of accuracy, reduce the tolerance to 0.5 percent.

**B Items:** +/− 3 percent. Since "B" items are lower in value or easier to get, the tolerances are set a little wider. If 1,000 parts are expected in the bin and 1,025 are found in the bin, if the item is classified a "B," the count would be considered accurate. If the item had been an "A," the count would be inaccurate. As these counts begin to stay within tolerance, decrease the tolerance limits.

**C Items:** +/− 5 percent. The "C" items are the lowest value of all and/or are very easy to replenish. The same part described before as having an inventory balance of 1,000 could have as many as 1,050 or as few as 950 and still be considered accurate. Another option for "C" items is to enter into a supplier partnership or simplify the overall ordering process. This change in focus guarantees availability of these parts without all the overhead of counting and issuing them. This process is used frequently with fasteners, shop supplies, safety supplies, and other MRO materials. The supplier can come directly into the plant like the legendary milkman and fill up any bin where parts have been used. This process eliminates the need for perpetual inventory control for these items.

Another option is to have a two-bin system, using the last bin to trigger the ordering process. The weakness in this method is that manual intervention must occur for the parts to be placed on order. The more reliable method is to have the supplier come directly into the plant and replenish these critical but bothersome supplies. Either of these simplified methods is excellent for parts that experience regular repetitive usage. When the environment is rapidly changing with respect to configuration and usage of these parts, shortages may result. As in any job, choosing the right tool simplifies the job.

Overall inventory record accuracy is calculated by adding all the accurate counts and dividing by the total number of counts performed. This is then expressed as a percentage. Inventory accuracy is not the percentage of parts found compared to the actual inventory. For example, a part is not 85 percent accurate if only 85 percent of the parts are found. That part would be 0 percent accurate. Inventory accuracy reflects the overall summary of "hits" and "misses." A hit is a count that falls within the defined tolerance, and a miss is a count that is outside the defined tolerance. The overall expectation for inventory accuracy is 100 percent. Realistically the process starts with wider tolerances until the overall accuracy increases into the 90 percent range, and then the tolerances are reduced. This will immediately reduce the overall accuracy, and continued process improvement will improve the results until again the results are in the 90 percent range. This closed-loop process continues until there is zero tolerance and the accuracy is in the 95 to 100 percent range. Significant energy and discipline are required to stay in this range. If you think that inventory accuracy is expensive, try inventory inaccuracy.

## EXPECTED RESULTS OF CYCLE COUNTING

Obviously the first expected result of cycle counting is accurate inventory balances. The investment required is minimal and can yield exceptional results that directly benefit the overall operation. One positive benefit is the elimination of the dreaded annual physical inventory. Even if the accounting firm thinks it needs an annual physical inventory, when it is shown that the annual physical inventory actually reduces inventory accuracy, it will quickly change its mind. Most accountants are reasonable people that just want to do a good job managing the overall financial results of the company. Cycle counting is consistent with that goal. Another benefit is that the cycle counting process as described is consistent with the closed-loop process improvement approach of the Shewhart "plan, do, check, act" cycle. Inventory accuracy is an easily measurable result for a cross-functional team that benefits the company directly. Imagine if there were never another inventory value writedown. Let's face it; those unexpected adjustments to inventory come directly out of the bottom line. Obviously the parts went somewhere. We may think we are making money on an order when we really are not due to the inventory that is used.

## SUMMARY

Inventory is the largest part of the current assets of the company. Keeping this asset accurate has many benefits throughout the business. The key for success in validating the inventory process is to develop a control group to identify process issues that affect overall inventory accuracy. Then, inventory accuracy results from discipline, discipline, discipline. The most accurate stockrooms are not necessarily the ones with the chainlink fences and barbed wire. Experience has shown that these stockrooms can be the least accurate, as people take great delight in circumventing the system to get parts. When you really look at it, what is it that production personnel really like to do? They enjoy shipping quality product to customers on time. They require parts to accomplish this mission. Locking these critical parts away in a high-security stockroom only frustrates these highly skilled people and leads to conflict with the storeroom personnel. Production people can be very creative in their attempts to get at the required parts. Why make it hard on them? The best process is one that is simple and easy to use, not difficult.

The overall inventory record accuracy effort should correct process issues, not just counts. Even though cycling through lots of numbers and correcting the database may look like good activity, it is not high productivity with any real value. The real goal is in correcting the process issues. An essential part is to feed back results to process owners. Overall inventory record accuracy should be collected and posted right in the stockroom area. Keeping the results in a book on a manager's desk does nothing to communicate progress. The results should be visible to everyone accountable and responsible for the inventory. This overall process might look like profound effort, but the benefits far exceed the cost. When the inventory records can be trusted, the results of the MRP system can also be trusted. This leads to significant inventory reduction. Inventory reduction makes it even easier to have accurate inventory records. This upward spiral delivers results monthly to the bottom line in terms of cash flow, profitability, and overall responsiveness to the customer. Unlike the chicken and the egg paradox, this spiral starts at a point, and that point is inventory accuracy. Even if the company has no plans to use MRP, the benefits of inventory accuracy include reduced non-value-added time doing things like verifying inventory before ordering or making customer service commitments. Communication is enhanced and work can be completed the first time. The alternative to validating the overall inventory process is not to bother. As the saying goes, "If you do what you have always done, you will get what you always got." In today's rapidly changing environment and high levels of growth of small companies, is that good enough?

With accurate input data, the planning and control function can focus on real operational issues. Many companies have attempted to leap to advanced systems like Just-In-Time (JIT) without having the strong foundation of data accuracy in place. Without this foundation, other systems are built on a house of cards that will easily collapse under the weight of normal operations and market changes.

# 6

MATERIALS REQUIREMENTS PLANNING (MRP)

## INTRODUCTION

During the mid-1960s, MRP was developed to help manufacturing companies increase their competitiveness. Interest in MRP has resumed lately because the increasing variety of products demanded by the customer and decreased product life cycles require increased vigilance for inventory management. The percentage of the cost of goods sold directly attributable to material mandates that effective inventory management is a core strategic issue for the company. The objective of MRP is to provide the right part, at the right time, at the right place. When run in its purest form without lot sizing, safety stock, and other inventory-building concepts, MRP looks much like JIT. Many people make MRP seem like a mystical entity that can solve all the business's problems or conversely cause all of the problems. MRP software programs are normally referred to simply as "the system." In discussions, the "system" takes on almost a human identity. When speaking about "the system," people usually have strong feelings, both positive and negative. Rarely does anyone stay in the middle of the road. With our affection for creative three-letter acronyms, MRP has come to mean many things in addition to its original intent.

The MRP system is not a mystical entity that can solve or cause all problems. MRP is a straightforward computer program that makes mathematical calculations. The program uses existing inventory data, determines the total requirements for each item, compares it to what is already on hand, and calculates what needs to be placed on order. This method of inventory control has been around for a long time. Project management is MRP for activities and materials. Even planning a birthday party can be considered MRP. First, the required finish date is set, and then all the activities required to make the party a success are planned. Invitations are sent out before the cake is ordered. The location must be determined before the invitations can be distributed. The idea of time-phasing materials and activities is a concept we use every day.

## MRP SYSTEM DEVELOPMENT

Detailed planning systems for manufacturing material came into being when computers were invented. Computers allowed detailed calculated projections of all component needs. The earliest MRP systems were written by computer manufacturers attempting to develop a market for their new product, the computer. Since those early days, there has been a fundamental change in the providers of computer software. Now, software companies focus on developing programs that fit the needs of specific industries and processes. Hardware companies form alliances and solutions partnerships with the software companies. Hardware has become more sophisticated and powerful and at the same time has decreased in price. The power of today's laptop computers exceeds the entire processing power of a university even 15 years ago. Software has become more user friendly and intuitive to use. Even with all the features and functions of modern computer systems, the reasons why the basic mathematical calculations of MRP are performed remain the same—What do I need, what do I have, what do I need to go get?

With MRP, the projected demand can be calculated in advance of the actual release of the work order. Since these dependent demands can be calculated, forecasting is not required. The calculations allow for highly accurate determination of need for the parts rather than the error-prone forecasting methods. No guessing is necessary. If the master production schedule states that 500 bicycles will be built on each of the next 10 consecutive Mondays, the MRP system will calculate the need for 1,000 wheels every Monday morning. Even though the sales of the bike are level each day, the demand for the wheels does not occur until Monday when the work order is released. This lumpiness of demand is a key characteristic of dependent demand items. Attempting to plan this material with an order point system, where parts are ordered when a minimum stocking level is reached, leads to sure disaster. Inventory remains with no use, only to experience sudden consumption in large quantities. The natural reaction is to increase inventory levels—a risky low return investment.

In the 1960s and 1970s, the logic of project management was applied to planning material. Just as a project plan requires all dependent activities to be completed before the next stage of the project can begin, MRP plans all materials to be available for the work order to begin. Project management tools have been in use for many years. Although the logic of project management existed many years before the first MRP systems were developed, the computational difficulty of applying it to smaller events prevented its widespread use for other applications. The advent of the computer allowed the same techniques to be applied to a smaller-scale project, an individual work order. Chapter 7 shows in detail how the MRP calculation is performed. Even with a small number of parts and a very shallow bill of materials, the calculations are quite extensive. Attempting to do these detailed calculations manually for a database of any size would take longer than to build the parts and does not add value to the process. The computer system provides detailed visibility that can be used to dramatically reduce the company's inventory investment. Many companies justify their entire implementation solely on the reduction of inventory.

## DEMAND PATTERNS

The real power of MRP is providing answers to the questions, How much and When? The way inventory was planned before the advent of MRP was to wait until a reorder point was reached, order the parts, and hope that the parts got there before running out. Unfortunately, the reorder point system works best for independent demand items, those items with demand coming from the exter-

nal customer. Independent demand tends to be relatively continuous and steady over a period of time. The overall demand for the
end item is level with some small level of variability. Inventory falls
in a steady predictable manner, as expected. Assuming that the
reorder point method for inventory replenishment is used, an order
is placed as the inventory drops to a predefined level. Reorder
points are marked with arrows in Figure 6–1.

**FIGURE   6–1**

Independent Demand Pattern

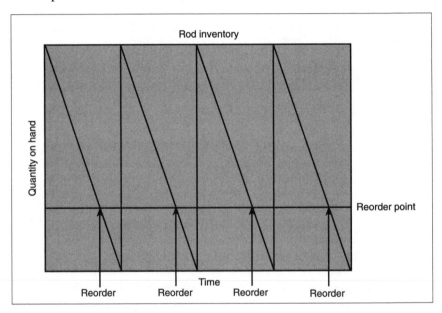

This type of demand pattern is considered a traditional sawtooth pattern. Inventory declines in an orderly fashion until the
order point is reached lead time away from the need. The replenishment arrives just as the inventory reaches zero. The average
inventory using this theory is the order quantity divided by two.
Typically the order quantity is fixed by part number and reflects
an economic quantity to produce or purchase.

Dependent demand—demand that arises from the need to build
the end item—is lumpy and discontinuous. This phenomenon

surprises many people until they look at it more closely. Demand for component parts does not exist until an order is released for the end item. At that time, there is a requirement for the parent's lot size quantity times the quantity for each item from the bill of material. If the product being built is fishing rods, there is no demand for reels until an order is released to build additional finished rods. If the order is for 500 rods, there is an instant demand for 500 reels all at once. Even though the independent demand for rods can be very level, say 50 per day, there is no demand for reels until the order is released to manufacture completed rods. The finished goods inventory has rods with reels attached. No additional reels are required until a manufacturing order is begun. When the manufacturing orders for rods are released, the result is simultaneous demand for all the components (bill of material quantity times the order quantity) to be available when the order is due to start. Figure 6–2 examines the effect on the demand for reels.

**F I G U R E    6–2**

Dependent Demand Pattern

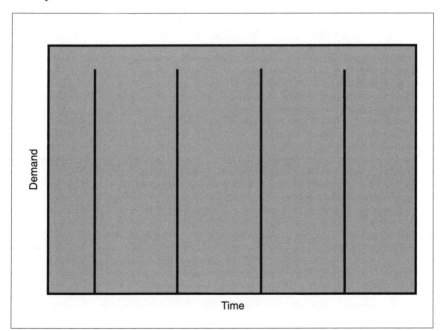

The demand arrives all at once, quickly depleting the available supply. This unexpected demand often causes expensive expediting as the supplying department or purchasing attempts to replenish the inventory. No visibility of declining inventory exists as in the order point system. Unlike the sawtooth shape of the independent demand graph, the graph of the demand for component items looks like discontinuous spikes. The reason is that all parts are required at the beginning of the process to start the order. Even though sales for the end item may be smooth and relatively continuous, demand for component inventory is affected by the parent's manufacturing lot size. The larger the lot size, the lumpier the demand is for component inventory. Figure 6–3 demonstrates the resulting inventory for reels given this spiky discontinuous demand.

Using reorder points to manage this type of inventory results in high levels of stockouts and a higher level of inventory overall. The inventory level drops all at once, triggering an order that is already too late. This is affectionately referred to as the OSWO (Oh Shoot We're Out) theory of inventory management. The natural reaction is to increase the level of inven-

FIGURE  6–3

Inventory Pattern for Dependent Demand Items

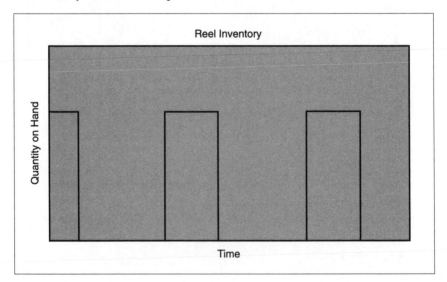

tory. On the other hand, simple logic says that when the parts are not required they should not be sitting in inventory. This use of company cash and other critical resources is wasted on inactive inventory. One way to minimize the lumpiness of demand is to reduce the lot size of production and/or procurement. This is the secret behind *kanban* pull replenishment systems. The lot sizes are so small and the replenishments occur so frequently that the lumpiness of dependent demand is not noticed. For traditional production, the lot size selected must allow efficient utilization of all company resources. Even though the inventory would be at a minimum if parts were ordered daily and built into finished goods daily, few companies have sufficient uniform demand to support this strategy of repetitive manufacturing. Another way is to order only what is needed, when it is needed. This is the basis and motivation for the development of MRP systems.

## SCHEDULING ALTERNATIVES

MRP plans all the items that have to be completed or purchased to support the master production schedule. The forward visibility allows the release of orders on time. This allows the planner to take on a proactive role in managing inventory. No longer is the inventory replenishment process reactive, waiting until a shortage occurs. Instead, requirements are projected; thus, replenishments can be planned and managed. There are some choices in scheduling the overall material and capacity needs.

### Backward Scheduling

Most commercially available MRP systems schedule events in a backward process. The master schedule date is taken as the end point, and then all components are offset backward through time by their respective lead times to determine the required completion and start dates for each. This type of logic is used in everyday life. When you determine when to get up in the morning, your thought process may be to work backward from when you want to be at work. Assuming that you are scheduled to start at 8 A.M. and have a 30-minute drive, you would leave your home at 7:30 A.M. Given that you like to eat breakfast and read the paper, which takes another 30 minutes, you know you should be ready by 7 A.M. If it takes one hour to get up and get ready for work, you set your alarm for 6 A.M. This kind of planning is done in many different daily activities. We make lists for what to take on vacation. All the items must be assembled before the vacation starts, similar to how all the components are required before a manufacturing work order can start. We do not have to physically go on vacation to be able to plan what is required and when. If we experience a shortage, the replacement can be costly and delay or damage the result of the vacation. In the same manner, a shortage in the production area can have far-reaching cost implications.

## Forward Scheduling

At times, scheduling forward rather than backward better meets the needs of the company. For example, if you get up late, say at 7 A.M., in your mind you quickly schedule things you must do to get to work. Given the same times as used in the backward scheduling example, the projected arrival time at work is 9 A.M. While this may be nice, it is not very practical. Suppose you really must get to work by 8 A.M. Some activities must be deleted or changed to accomplish the expedited schedule. You may forgo reading the newspaper and eat your breakfast on the drive to work.

Using this same technique, many companies plan for the soonest time that a part can be completed using forward scheduling. If the resulting date is not acceptable, the sequence and duration of events, both value added and queue, are reviewed and adjusted until either there is no additional time that can be taken out or the desired date has been reached. In the example used of getting to work, sometimes things are done that seem to expedite the process but in the long run defeat the purpose. Getting to work sooner by speeding may seem like a good idea at the time until the local law enforcement officer intercedes. The time it takes to get a ticket offsets dramatically any perceived time savings accomplished through speeding. Similarly, attempting to speed selected items through the plant results in similar negative repercussions. The attempt may make sense at the time, and sometimes you actually get away with it. But when done routinely, in the long run you will always get caught.

## PLANNING THE UNKNOWN

Many people believe that plans can only be developed for parts that have been built before. Just as estimates and road maps can be used when going someplace new, parts can be effectively planned without having actually built them before. By making estimates of lead time, the overall start and stop dates and material requirements can be calculated. How many of us could afford to take a trial vacation just to ensure that we did the planning correctly for the real one? The same situation exists in the Production Planning area.

The powerful tool of MRP allows us to plan many parts with many interrelationships. MRP is not magic, just a big calculator for dependent demand to provide visibility of overall requirements in advance of the event. The biggest advantage of an MRP implementation is that inventory is planned to arrive just when it is needed. This minimizes inventory and the accompanying carrying cost and expense. In fact, many MRP implementations are cost justified on the reduction of inventory alone. For all these benefits, the requirements are really quite simple.

## MRP SYSTEM REQUIREMENTS

### Master Production Schedule

A master production schedule is required to drive the material requirements planning system. The master schedule contains items that are fully defined in bill of material terms. The master schedule is a statement of what is planned to be completed by defining quantities and timing for each parent item. The bills of material define the components for each parent. The two items together are critical to calculating the part's requirements. The master schedule answers the question of how much and when. The bill of material answers the question of what. MRP uses these two inputs to calculate how much, what, and when.

## Inventory Records

Every inventory item that will be stocked must be identified uniquely and have an inventory record available. Inventory records include information about:

- **On hand**: How many parts are currently in inventory, available for use.

- **On order**: How many parts have already been ordered from the supplier (either internal or external) and when they are due to arrive.

- **Lead time**: How long the replenishment is expected to take from the time of order. A common error is not to include the amount of time it takes to place the item on order. Some companies requiring three quotations and awarding the purchase to the lowest bidder can use significant lead time in this process. The amount of time required to receive and inspect the parts must also be included. If only the supplier's lead time is used, the parts always will be late.

- **Planning data**: These factors define the order sizes and timing. This can include lot sizing rules such as lot for lot, economic order quantities, order minimums/ maximums/multiples, and period of supply. These tools are detailed in later chapters.

## Unique Item Identification

MRP plans by unique items. Having multiple identifications for a part because there are multiple suppliers will not allow MRP to add the requirements for this part together and suggest the best order quantity possible. Defining the identification system can evoke many opinions and emotions. The best systems have concise part numbers containing all numeric digits (i.e., nonsignificant codes). The most common error is to encode descriptive information into the part number (i.e., significant codes). The belief is that this will help the shop floor find things and make the system easier to use. The opposite often is true. For example, 123278125 could be a significant code for a guide for a fishing rod.

The first two digits 12 denote the manufacturer. The next three digits are a color key. The last four digits are the model for which the parts are usually purchased. Unless all the translations for the codes are known, this just looks like a very long part number. The chances that the entire part number will be used on a daily basis is minimal. The people using the numbers always find some way to shorten them to a useable length.

The only people that the significant part number assists are the people who designed it. The encoding of information requires a translation key and soon the code is forgotten, leaving long part numbers in use with no benefit. Having short numeric part identifiers allows the users to remember and use the correct identifier for the correct part. The real function of the part number is to uniquely identify the part. Additional functionality of the software allows the other information to be attributed to the part in a simpler fashion.

Studies have shown that the chance of repeating the entry of a number with more than seven digits falls to zero quickly. There seems to be no significant difference between six and seven digits, presumably because of the phone number recall ability for most people. In small businesses, the need for a part number in excess of five digits is rare. Five numeric digits allow the company to have 99,999 part numbers. Even if the five-digit number starts with 10,000, the possibility exists for 90,000 part numbers. This is sufficient to support a company up to $30 million in revenue! The advantages of nonsignificant part numbers are that they are easier to enter and recall. Accuracy of the inventory is usually better with a shorter number. The company is also poised to support future growth. If all five digits are used up, a sixth can be easily added. The main disadvantages of significant part numbers are that they are longer and the company can easily run out of numbers depending on the coding scheme. Introductions of unexpected new products can throw the entire system into chaos. Usually the floor personnel begin using only a short subset of the number to identify the part, or worse, they rename it to something that makes sense for them. This quickly results in confusion, incorrect part use, and errors in inventory data. Don't be fooled into thinking that bar codes will eliminate this problem. Someone still has to look at and pick those parts with the long number. Part numbers are used for many things in addition to data entry. They are the basis of the language of the MRP system.

In either case, the inventory records define all the characteristics of the parts. If the company wishes to stock a part and/or collect information about a part, a unique number is used. The best rule of thumb is that if there is a change in fit, form, or function, a new part number is required. If a blindfolded person cannot use any part in the bin, a new part number is needed.

## OBTAINING QUALITY OUTPUT

With only these three requirements—a master production schedule stated in bill of material terms, unique part numbers, and inventory data—any MRP system will run. Notice that nothing has been mentioned yet about the quality and accuracy of the inputs. Many people like to blame "the system" when the information they receive as output is wrong. In reality, the inputs are normally the problem. Since users expect high-quality results from their system, high-quality inputs are required. Remember the adage, "You can't make a silk purse out of a sow's ear." The key inputs to obtaining high-quality output follow.

### Accurate File Data

File data must be accurate. This includes on-hand balances, bills of material, part numbers, planning data, schedules, and everything else that is an input in the system. Accuracy in the master schedule means that the schedule is realistic and doable. The master schedule should be a stretch but not impossible. Since MRP starts the calculation with how many are on hand, inventory record accuracy is essential. Bills of material drive the entire calculation process to determine requirement quantities. The parent–component relationships must be an accurate reflection of the part and quantity used or shortages or excess inventory will result. Inaccuracy of input data is the most common reason for failure of MRP system implementations.

### Realistic Lead Times

MRP treats lead times as fixed. Due to expediting and priority changes, lead times can change based on the time of year or month. The end of the month in most manufacturing companies results in shorter-than-expected manufacturing lead times as parts are expedited to completion to achieve monthly revenue goals. Close estimates are good enough for a successful system. Lead time is one area where a conservative estimate will result in excellent part availability. As the MRP process becomes more fine tuned in the efforts of continuous improvement and inventory declines, more accurate lead times are required to prevent inventory from arriving too early or too late.

## Inventory Transactions

Every inventory item is transacted into and out of stock as required. At each level of the bill of material, work orders must be opened, component parts issued, and finished goods received. This is not to say that completed subassemblies must physically move into and out of a stockroom. Some of the most accurate stockrooms are in the middle of the shop floor. Accuracy does not come from chainlink fences and padlocks. Accuracy comes from *discipline* concerning the inventory consumption transactions. This discipline cannot be stressed enough. If the on-hand balance is incorrect, poor schedules and priorities are a guaranteed result from the MRP run.

## Order Independence

MRP schedules to have all components available for the start date of the manufacturing order. Orders should not have to wait for parts or people when planning has been done effectively and implementation is well disciplined. For maximum production efficiency, all the parts must be available when the order is begun. An excellent discipline is that no work order should be released short parts. When shortages are allowed onto the shop floor, the downward spiral is hard to stop. Tracking partial orders consumes a significant amount of resources. The result is high work in process and usually late orders, as extensive labor and cash resources are spent attempting to relieve the shortages. Just finding the order after it has been set aside because of a shortage can be a challenge. The resource is better spent building quality product and delivering it to the customer.

## MRP OUTPUT

The result of the MRP explosion is a schedule of order actions and messages by exception. The MRP process matches the part requirements with incoming parts or on-hand quantities. MRP outputs notify the planner of problems and actions. The planner takes action on these messages to bring the production and inventory planning back into balance. Planner messages are to release orders to buy, make, cancel, or reschedule based on the current conditions. Changes are easily incorporated through this plan by exception process. The key point is that the underlying cause for the imbalance must be addressed and resolved. Just deleting planner messages does not make them go away. The same messages will be back the next time MRP is run. If you do not like the output, challenge the inputs. The problem (and solution) will be found there.

**F I G U R E   6–4**

Manufacturing Tickler Report

Buyer/Planner: Sara

| Item ID | Item Name | Ref. | Code | U M | Required Quantity | Required Date |
|---|---|---|---|---|---|---|
| **Late** | | | | | | |
| 89547 | Sportsman's special rod | 1003 | WO | Each | 5.00 | 12/15/95 |
| | | 1011 | WO | Each | 9.00 | 12/22/95 |
| | | 1014 | WO | Each | 25.00 | 12/15/95 |
| **Short/Increase** | | | | | | |
| 89547 | Sportsman's special rod | 1009 | WO | Each | 500.00 | 4/1/96 |
| **Short/Order** | | | | | | |
| 12054 | Custom configuration rod | Pat | END | Each | 160.00 | 1/15/96 |
| 25377 | Bass rod | cap | END | Each | 62.00 | 1/15/96 |
| 34926 | Blank, rod, graphite | 89547 | WO | Each | 529.00 | 1/17/96 |
| **Slide** | | | | | | |
| 89547 | Sportsman's special rod | 1003 | WO | Each | 5.00 | 12/15/95=> 1/1/96 |

The manufacturing tickler report in Figure 6–4 shows the type of exception reporting that can be expected from a working MRP system. No longer must the planner look at every part individually or react only when inventory is depleted. Only parts with imbalances and other problems must be addressed. The planners then assemble their pieces of the puzzle to support the company's overall objectives and strategy.

## SUMMARY

MRP systems were developed in response to a real need in manufacturing companies. Independent demand could be handled with simple order point systems. Dependent demand was an entirely different matter. Excess inventory had to be carried to service the sudden surges of component demand. Project management tools were applied to this problem with the arrival of powerful computer systems. Now materials could be planned to be available when the order was due to start without carrying excess inventory.

The sophisticated computer systems also provide scheduling alternatives. Material schedules can be developed from a completion date. The system calculates backward from the required date for materials to support the finished product. The other alternative, forward scheduling, calculates the earliest the part can be completed, given standard lead times. This sophisticated planning can occur for parts that have never been made before, given just a few simple data elements. These include a master schedule stated in bill of material terms, inventory records available for all parts, and uniquely identified parts.

To obtain quality output, however, some additional items are added. The focus on the quality and accuracy of the input data is the key success factor in an MRP implementation. This includes all inventory transactions completed in a timely manner and realistic lead time estimates for all parts. Another success factor is the release of orders *only* when all the parts are available. The result of all this hard work is visibility of what needs to be ordered, rescheduled, or expedited to meet the top-level master production schedule. Not only does MRP plan what is required and in what quantity, but the real power is that MRP answers the question of "when" in a proactive way. The benefit to the company is dramatic decreases in inventory and improved profitability.

# 7

⑥  MRP SYSTEM
DEFINITION REFINEMENTS

## INTRODUCTION

As discussed in Chapter 6, many companies and practitioners behave as if an MRP system is a magical entity. Some companies discuss the "system" as if it is living and has a personality. MRP is a relatively simple mathematical calculation of parts required based on the given schedule, bills of material, and current inventory. Knowing how the computer does its calculations allows the user to better understand the output. This understanding allows the user to troubleshoot any unexpected output by examining the appropriate inputs. The real purpose of MRP is to balance the demand and supply. The system looks at what is needed, deducts what is in inventory and on order, and plans the difference to be available when needed. The mind-boggling part is that it efficiently projects these differences into the future for many, many parts.

The need that MRP was developed to serve is that dependent demand inventory cannot be effectively managed using simple order point techniques. The unique demand pattern of dependent demand inventory defies prediction by the order point method. When an order is released to the manufacturing factory to build parts, one of the assumptions is that all component parts will be available. Having all the parts when the order is released leads to improved manufacturing efficiency, less expediting, and higher quality. Even though the demand for the end item can be relatively continuous, there is no demand for the components until the work order replenishing the end item supply is released. This supply work order is released one total lead time ahead of the net requirement for the part. The larger and less frequent the orders are for the parent part, the lumpier is the demand for its components. The smaller and more regular the orders are for the parent part, the more regular and level is the demand for the components. Since most small companies make to a larger company's order, the demand for the parent part is usually relatively lumpy and discontinuous. The part may be built only once. The resulting lumpy demand for the parent item leads to even lumpier demand for the component materials. In some cases there may be reorders for a batch of the same part for the customer at some future date.

The need for effectively planning dependent demand is especially great in small businesses. The focus on cash flow and the need for the optimal utilization of all resources is especially high in small business. Having too much or too little inventory can put a small company out of business quickly. Too much inventory consumes critical company resources. Too little inventory can create a shortage for the customer and no incoming revenue. Understanding and effectively utilizing the tools of MRP enhances the profitability and efficiency of the small business.

## MRP—A CLOSER LOOK

The requirements and assumptions of an MRP system have already been discussed. This section will take a close look at the planning process using MRP. A planning time period can be a day, a week, or a month. Most companies plan their MRP systems in terms of days, with some planning in weekly buckets. The monthly bucket is not sufficiently detailed to provide worthwhile information. Modern systems plan in a bucketless format that can display in any desired time format or bucket size. Each independent demand item is planned, and requirements are defined for lower-level components. Demand is accumulated for any components used by more than one top-level part. Once all the demand is calculated for the component part, then the replenishments are planned based on what is already in inventory and on order. This process continues through the levels of the bill of material to all component parts. Remember that MRP plans all materials to be available just when they are needed and not before. A common misconception is that MRP will plan materials to be available a period before they are required to provide safety time in case something goes wrong. This is absolutely wrong. MRP plans everything to be available only when it is needed, not before and not after. Think of Goldilocks and the Three Bears—MRP is not too early, not too late, but just on time. This explains why the lead times identified for each part must be a conservative yet realistic estimate.

## Gross to Net Calculation

Bill of material for part A

  A
  . B (1)
  . C (2)
  .. B (2)
  .. D (3)

This bill of material means that one part B and two part Cs are used to build each part A. In turn, two part Bs and three part Ds are used to build each C. Considering the position in the bill of material and assuming that the bill has been completely structured with all its parts, parts B and D are purchased. Parts A and C are manufactured. The desire is to plan all requirements for part B once. The figures that follow describe how MRP calculates the demand for all parts.

  Table 7–1 demonstrates the MRP standard calculations for the two make parts. The gross requirements for item C are exactly double the expected order release for item A. The timing of the requirement is exactly when the order for A is expected to be released. Remember that one of the assumptions of MRP is that all materials will be available at the time of order release. In this example, both parts use a fixed order quantity. This choice will be further described later in this chapter.

TABLE 7-1

MRP Example

**Item ID: A**
Lot size=400, Low Lvl=0, OH=300
LT=1, Alloc=0, SS=150

|                        | 1   | 2   | 3   | 4   | 5   | 6   | 7   | 8   |
| ---------------------- | --- | --- | --- | --- | --- | --- | --- | --- |
| Master Schedule        | 100 | 400 | 200 | 300 | 100 | 200 | 300 | 100 |
| Scheduled Receipts     | 400 |     |     |     |     |     |     |     |
| Projected on Hand      | 600 | 200 | 400 | 500 | 400 | 200 | 300 | 200 |
| Planned Order Receipts |     |     | 400 | 400 |     |     | 400 |     |
| Planned Order Releases |     | 400 | 400 |     |     | 400 |     |     |

**Item ID: C**

Lot size=500, Low Lvl=2, OH=1500
LT=2, Alloc=0, SS=100

|                        | 1     | 2   | 3   | 4   | 5   | 6   | 7   | 8   |
| ---------------------- | ----- | --- | --- | --- | --- | --- | --- | --- |
| Gross Requirements     |       | 800 | 800 |     |     | 800 |     |     |
| Scheduled Receipts     |       |     |     |     |     |     |     |     |
| Projected on Hand      | 1,500 | 700 | 400 | 400 | 400 | 100 | 100 | 100 |
| Planned Order Receipts |       |     | 500 |     |     | 500 |     |     |
| Planned Order Releases | 500   |     |     | 500 |     |     |     |     |

Now the system can explode the requirements from these two make parts to the purchased parts. Demand for B comes from two parent items, first from the demand for A, as shown in Table 7–2. This places requirements for 400 in periods 2, 3, and 6. The demands for 1,000 in periods 1 and 4 come from the

**T A B L E   7–2**

MRP Example: Dependent Demand

**Item ID: B**
Lot size=LFL, Low Lvl=2, OH=2,000
LT=3, Alloc=0, SS=200

|  | 1 | 2 | 3 | 4 | 5 | 6 | 7 | 8 |
|---|---|---|---|---|---|---|---|---|
| Gross Requirements | 1,000 | 400 | 400 | 1,000 |  | 400 |  |  |
| Scheduled Receipts |  |  |  |  |  |  |  |  |
| Projected on Hand | 1,000 | 600 | 200 | 200 | 200 | 200 | 200 | 200 |
| Planned Order Receipts |  |  |  | 1,000 |  |  | 400 |  |
| Planned Order Releases | 1,000 |  | 400 |  |  |  |  |  |

**Item ID: D**

Lot size=LFL, Low Lvl=2, OH=1675
LT=3, Alloc=100, SS=0, Scrap=10%

|  | 1 | 2 | 3 | 4 | 5 | 6 | 7 | 8 |
|---|---|---|---|---|---|---|---|---|
| Gross Requirements | 1,500 |  |  | 1,500 |  |  |  |  |
| Scheduled Receipts | 225 |  |  |  |  |  |  |  |
| Projected on Hand | 300 | 300 | 300 | 0 | 0 | 0 | 0 | 0 |
| Planned Order Receipts |  |  |  | 1,200 |  |  |  |  |
| Planned Order Releases | 1,334 |  |  |  |  |  |  |  |

explosion from C through the bill of material that calls out 2 each for item B. The MRP system can then plan the net requirements for product B, 1,000 in period 4 and 400 in period 6. These net requirements are backward offset for estimated lead time to yield planned order releases in periods 1 and 3.

Notice that even though the planning horizon is still eight periods, the last requirement for item D is only in period 4. Having the master schedule input for some time into the future is essential. The total time required for the master schedule is dependent on the parent item overall cumulative lead time. This cumulative lead time must include the time to place orders, receive parts, inspect parts, put parts away and issue them on pick lists for individual manufacturing orders and, finally, to make the top assembly. In other words, the total cumulative lead time must take into account all the time required to make the end item, including all the raw material, component parts, and processes. This is not the lead time that is in the end item definition for planning work orders. The lead time in the item master is only the amount of time required to build the end item from its first-level components. This lead time assumes that all parts are available when the order is released. The total cumulative lead time includes the longest time for all component parts added together following the bill of material process definition.

If the master schedule is input for only the minimum length of time, the purchasing planners will always be placing orders for purchased parts at the last minute. The farther out a master schedule can be confidently entered into the future can benefit the company in purchasing's ability to combine order quantities and order materials on a blanket order with multiple releases. This usually reduces the price of the material. Given that the largest part of the cost of goods sold is material, the ability to reduce the material expense by a small percentage can increase the overall profitability of the company. For example, as shown in Chapter 1, if material is 60 percent of the cost of goods sold, a 10 percent reduction in material cost will increase profit to the company by 18 percent. This forward visibility is essential for effective management of material purchases.

### Low-Level Coding

What happens if the same part is used in two different bills of material or twice in the same bill of material? The MRP calculation adds the requirements from both sources and plans orders to cover the total requirements. Part B in the previous example experiences this kind of demand, as shown in Table 7–3.

TABLE   7–3

Low-Level Coding Effect

**Item ID: B**
Lot size=LFL, Low Lvl=2, OH=2,000
LT=3, Alloc=0, SS=200

| | 1 | 2 | 3 | 4 | 5 | 6 | 7 | 8 |
|---|---|---|---|---|---|---|---|---|
| Gross Requirements | 1,000 | 400 | 400 | 1,000 | | 400 | | |
| Scheduled Receipts | | | | | | | | |
| Projected on Hand | 1,000 | 600 | 200 | 200 | 200 | 200 | 200 | 200 |
| Planned Order Receipts | | | | 1,000 | | 400 | | |
| Planned Order Releases | 1,000 | | 400 | | | | | |

In periods 1 and 4, the 1000 piece gross requirements come from the demand to build part C. For each C built, there is a requirement for 2 part Bs. The orders for C are planned for release in periods 1 and 4. All materials are planned to be available at time of the order release. Similarly, the demands in periods 2, 3, and 6 come from the demand for item A. Only 1 B is required for each A. Again, the timing of the requirement for B matches the planned released for A. Once all the gross requirements are known, MRP can plan the expected order releases for part B. Since the lot size rule for B is lot for lot or discrete order quantity, only what is needed is planned to be ordered. The safety stock of 200 is planned as the minimum inventory needed on hand. These two factors working together yield a plan for orders for B to be released in periods 1 and 3. Since there is visibility of the future need of 400 in period 6 when the order is released for period 1, the buyer/planner would most likely release one order for 1400 with two scheduled receipts, one in period 4 for 1000 pieces and one in period 6 for 400 pieces. This combination of orders for purchased parts saves paperwork and cost. In addition, the scheduled deliveries provide excellent visibility for the supplier.

The common parts were not at the same level of the bill of material. How did the MRP system know to wait for all the demands to be accumulated? All MRP systems use a process called low-level coding to ensure that each part is run only once with all requirements being considered. This technique also makes computer processing more efficient. Each item is considered only once at the lowest place (highest number level) it occurs in any bill of material. The low-level code is assigned and maintained by the computer. By processing each item in turn, at the lowest level it occurs, total requirements and replenishment orders will be calculated accurately, giving realistic planner messages. The low-level codes are displayed in the part information in the example provided. The computer system itself calculates these codes for its own processing. No human intervention is required or allowed.

## Exception Messages

The master production schedule is exploded through the bills of material to give the user exception messages. These exception messages include rescheduling (in and out), release orders, or cancel orders. The underlying condition must be corrected for the exception message to disappear. The first messages to be addressed should be the order cancellations. This minimizes the cash flow impact and does not build potentially obsolete inventory. The next priority is to reschedule parts. After the reschedules are completed, then the new order releases should be handled. Sometimes the new order releases can be worked in conjunction with the rescheduling messages so that each part is examined and worked only one. Different systems handle the MRP explosion in different ways. Refer to your system's specific user manuals to determine the immediacy of the impact of order changes. Some systems will re-explode down one level and will show the effect immediately of rescheduling, cancellations, or opening orders on the parent and its first-level components. Most systems will require a net change run to fully see the impact of these schedule changes. Modern systems have developed quicker methods for this net change calculation. Some companies are beginning to perform this net change during the lunch break to allow the planners maximum visibility and feedback on changes made elsewhere in the system. In small companies, typically there are a small number of planners and the replanning can be done quite easily. Daily replanning is usually sufficient to provide adequate visibility.

## Pegging

Resolving imbalances requires knowing the source of the requirement. The MRP explosion also allows the user to peg—to find out why there is a requirement for a part by moving up the bill of materials. Table 7–4 is an example of a pegging report.

The important thing to remember about pegging is that only sources of demand are shown from which requirements are coming. The where used report shows all the places the component is used. The pegging report only shows those that have requirements. The pegging report, an essential tool in every planner's toolbox, is further discussed in Chapter 8.

**T A B L E   7–4**

Pegging Report

| Item ID:<br>43086<br>Item Name:<br>Graphite, prepreg | | On Hand Quantity: 400.00<br>Non Net Quantity: 0.00<br>Safety Stock: 100.00<br>Lead Time Code: Purchased | | | Order Policy: Min/Max<br>PO Inspect Qty: 0.00<br>WIP Inspect Qty: 0.00<br>Lead Time: 35 | |
|---|---|---|---|---|---|---|
| Qty/Assy:<br>Unit Measure: | 6.0000<br>Lin. Yd. | Date | Type | Reference | In | Out |
| | | 12/7/95 | | | | |
| | | | RQ | source-34926, 12/28/95 | | 50 |
| | | 2/10/96 | | | | |
| | | | PO | 96002, 1 | 50.00 | |
| | | 3/10/96 | | | | |
| | | | PO | 96002, 1 | 75.00 | |
| | | 12/15/96 | | | | |
| | | | PO | 96005, 1 | 3.00 | |

## NET CHANGE/REGENERATIVE MRP

Two different approaches are used to explode the schedule: net change or regenerative. Net change only recalculates the requirements for those items where there has been an unexpected change. This triggering is accomplished by a flag being set whenever an unplanned transaction occurs on the part. If the receipts and issues of the part are according to plan, no explosion of the part will be triggered. Only when the activity of the part is not according to plan are the part and its components recalculated by MRP.

The other process of calculating the requirements is regenerative MRP. This process is a clean sweep. The entire old schedule is deleted and a new one is recalculated. Don't worry: existing orders are not deleted; they are reevaluated against the schedule requirements, and exception messages are generated if planner action is recommended.

Each method has its advantages and disadvantages. The advantages of a net change system include shorter run time that allows more frequent replanning. This can also be a disadvantage to the planner who cannot respond to all the planner messages before the next run is completed. However, any message not handled is back on the next run. Usually the net change system has some auxiliary process that picks up those issues that arise only due to the passage of time, including late orders. The main advantage of a regenerative system is that the computer programming is very simple. No distinction must be made between parts to consider in the MRP process. The disadvantage is that processing the entire database can take an extremely long time. The power of modern computers is making this time shrink dramatically.

The explosion method selected is based on the business environment. If the business is very dynamic with frequent bills of material and schedule changes, net change MRP runs daily should be used. Conversely, if the business is static with few changes, a weekly regenerative run can be used. Modern MRP systems allow a choice of either. The net change MRP process including all parts is a regenerative run. Usually the regenerative run takes longer. However, with the improved processing speeds on today's computers, this is no longer a main concern. The rule of thumb is to run the MRP batch calculation as frequently as the planners can respond to the resulting planner messages.

## LOT SIZING

Another tool that planners use is lot sizing. Rarely is the quantity of materials ordered exactly equal to the requirements. Usually extra quantities are purchased to take advantage of price breaks, minimum order sizes, or packaging conventions. On the manufacturing side, order quantities can be used for tools that make multiple parts. Fixed order quantities can be scheduled because of cost considerations and process limitations. This recognizes the trade-off in cost between carrying inventory and spreading the cost of a long setup over a larger run of parts.

Different lot size methods used are lot for lot (LFL), economic order quantity (EOQ), order minimum, order maximum, order multiple, and period of supply (POS). Most MRP systems support all these different lot sizing rules.

### Lot for Lot (LFL or Discrete)

This order quantity is the simplest of the lot sizing rules. This lot quantity has no increase in the order quantity compared to the net required quantity. When the rule of lot for lot is followed, only the amount of material needed is ordered, no more, no less. Lot for lot is usually the default lot quantity for MRP systems. This lot size is most appropriate for make-to-order work. Even though it is the simplest to understand, this method creates the most orders. Each requirement for a component material is matched with a corresponding order. The benefit of this method is that inventory is minimized. Table 7–5 shows the result of lot for lot for part A. The planned order releases exactly equal the net requirements offset by the planned lead time.

### Economic Order Quantity

This lot sizing choice recognizes the trade-off between the cost of carrying inventory and the cost to set up a machine. The same

**TABLE 7-5**

Lot-for-Lot (Discrete) Order Quantity

| Item ID: A<br>Lot size=LFL, Low Lvl=0, OH=300<br>LT=1, Alloc=0, SS=150 | 1 | 2 | 3 | 4 | 5 | 6 | 7 | 8 |
|---|---|---|---|---|---|---|---|---|
| Master Schedule | 100 | 400 | 200 | 300 | 100 | 200 | 300 | 100 |
| Scheduled Receipts | 400 | | | | | | | |
| Projected on Hand | 600 | 200 | 150 | 150 | 150 | 150 | 150 | 150 |
| Planned Order Receipts | | | 150 | 300 | 100 | 200 | 300 | 100 |
| Planned Order Releases | | 150 | 300 | 100 | 200 | 300 | 100 | |

logic is applied to purchase orders comparing the cost of carrying inventory with the cost of placing the purchase orders. As more inventory is carried, the cost of carrying that inventory goes up proportionately. On the other hand, manufacturing favors long runs to spread the cost of the setup. This method leads to higher inventories. The economic order quantity, although very old, is still used to determine the order of magnitude of the optimal order size. Many people get carried away with the EOQ formula and attempt to apply it inappropriately. EOQ still has a fit in the business process that experiences long setup times and comparatively shorter run times. The business must need all the parts calculated by the EOQ. If the company has only make-to-order demand and the EOQ calculates a lot quantity higher than the demand, those extra parts should not be made just for the sake of EOQ. EOQ is an approximation of the order quantity. The calculation gives the appearance of precision, but the resulting order quantity is really just a guideline. The total cost does not change very much around the EOQ quantity. Other components might be better served to use other order rules.

The EOQ formula is $\sqrt{\dfrac{2US}{IC}}$, where:

U = annual expected usage in units.

S = setup cost in dollars.

I = inventory carrying cost expressed as an annual percentage.

C = the cost of the item in dollars.

The resulting order quantity will be in units of production.

U:   The annual expected usage in units either can be the historic consumption of the past year or the forecast usage based on the master schedule for the upcoming year.

S:   The setup cost in dollars includes all the costs associated with changing from one production run to another. Setup time can be considered as the time from the last good part of the previous run to the first good part of the next run. All costs associated with that time and procedure should be included in the setup costs. Usually these times are estimated in terms of hours of production and are costed by applying a standard labor rate for the area and adding overhead burden. For purchased parts these costs include the entire order preparation cost for the purchasing department. The costs are generated for each purchase order as it moves through the receipt process, receiving inspection, storage, and invoice payment. The traditional approach is to add all these overhead costs and divide by the number of purchase orders issued during that time period. The caution is that some purchase orders take significantly more time than others. For the purposes of calculating the economic order quantity, the average is sufficient.

I:   The inventory carrying cost is one of the most difficult costs to determine. The most frequent way this cost is determined is by asking the head of the finance department. This person usually has some strong feelings concerning the value of the money currently tied up in inventory. A rough estimation can be made by adding the cost of borrowing money to the cost of running the warehouse, including the people, computer systems, and floor space. Other factors to be included in the cost of carrying inventory are the risk of obsolescence, damage, theft, or spoilage. The largest part of the inventory carrying cost is the opportunity cost of that money. Opportunity cost is what the yield could be if the money were not tied up in inventory. This can be significant in an entrepreneurial business that has the potential to grow quickly. After all quantitative factors are considered, the norm for inventory carrying costs is in the range of 40 to 70 percent per year.

C:   The cost of the item used in the EOQ formula is usually the fully loaded cost, including overhead, used to value the inventory for bookkeeping purposes. These costs include material, labor, overhead, and outside production services.

There are some underlying assumptions to the EOQ formula. The first is that inventory is consumed at a regular and continuous rate. This assumption supports the belief that the average inventory is half the order quantity. Remember the discussion in Chapter 6 about the behavior of independent and dependent demand inventory. This is where the "2" comes from in the formula. Realistically, inventory is consumed in a company in a lumpy, noncontinuous way. When dependent demand is considered, the consumption pattern is anything but regular and continuous. The difficulty in managing this type of demand pattern is the reason MRP was developed. The other underlying assumptions that are questionable are that the inventory carrying cost can be accurately estimated and that the number is realistic. In small companies, this estimation usually is a reflection of the cash position of the company—the tighter the cash supply, the higher the cost of inventory. When the cost of inventory is fully considered, the largest component of that cost is the opportunity cost for the money tied up in inventory. Opportunity cost is defined as the best possible return on that money if it was not invested in inventory. Small businesses often have excellent growth opportunities but are constrained in their growth by the availability of resources, usually cash.

On the subject of cost, typically companies calculate the overhead rate based on the expected budget for overhead activities divided by the number of expected production hours. Knowing that the first rule of forecasting is that forecasts are always wrong places some doubt on this exact calculation of overhead. The overhead number is considered a best guess. Knowing that this guess can affect the cost of the item as well as the setup cost, the computational precision of the EOQ is somewhat in question. The forecast of the annual usage suffers from the same issue as the forecast of the overhead cost per hour. When all these limitations are taken into account, you might wonder how the EOQ became so popular. The mathematical computation is really based on some rocky assumptions. The precision that results from using this formula is quite an illusion. Drastic changes can be made in each of the components with little difference in the optimal order quantity. The real application of the EOQ is to determine the order of magnitude of the optimal order quantity, not the exact quantity; for example, should you order 100 or 1,000, not 100 or 110? Table 7–6 clearly shows how the economic order quantity changes significantly less than the selected input. The annual usage

**T A B L E   7–6**

EOQ Sensitivity

| Annual Usage | Setup Cost | Inventory Carrying Cost | Cost of the Item | Quantity (EOQ) | Percent EOQ | Change Usage |
|---|---|---|---|---|---|---|
| 1000 | $1,000 | 40% | $250 | 141 | | |
| 2500 | $1,000 | 40% | $250 | 224 | 58% | 150% |
| 5000 | $1,000 | 40% | $250 | 316 | 41% | 100% |
| **Annual Usage** | **Setup Cost** | **Inventory Carrying Cost** | **Cost of the Item** | **Quantity (EOQ)** | **Percent EOQ** | **Change Carrying Cost** |
| 2500 | $1,000 | 30% | $250 | 258 | | |
| 2500 | $1,000 | 40% | $250 | 224 | −13% | 33% |
| 2500 | $1,000 | 60% | $250 | 183 | −18% | 50% |

increased by 150 percent and the EOQ increased only 58 percent. When the carrying cost for inventory was doubled, the EOQ only decreased 18 percent. This shows that best estimates can be used for each of the inputs without adversely affecting the accuracy of the output. The planner can adjust order quantities around the EOQ without suffering a significant cost penalty.

Since the main driving force behind lot size is setup cost, the focus for process improvement should be on reducing the setup cost. Once the setup cost is reduced, smaller lot sizes can be run. Smaller lot sizes result in lower inventories. Lower inventories typically yield higher profit and better responsiveness to the market. This responsiveness is a key competitive edge for the small business. Typically, small business is more nimble and responsive to the market than large bureaucratic companies. Being able to build smaller lot sizes in a cost-effective manner enhances this nimble responsiveness.

## Order Minimum/Multiple/Maximum

When purchasing parts, sometimes there is an order minimum set by the supplier. Rather than having MRP plan frequent orders less than this minimum quantity, the order minimum plans the order quantity to be at least the known minimum. If the needed order quantity is greater than the minimum, the quantity planned will match the requirement if no other lot sizing rule is defined.

Order multiple takes advantage of natural order quantities due to production batch size, such as a full oven load for heat treat or a multiple cavity die. Suppliers may deliver parts in cases that are subsequently stored as "each" by the customer. This could be cases of fasteners, gloves, or adhesives. Orders to the supplier must be in case quantities or multiples of the "each" that will eventually be stored. If the quantity required is less than a multiple of the specified amount, the order quantity planned will be automatically increased to the next higher multiple.

Order maximum may be used because of a limitation of space or restriction on the amount of the product that can be transported or stored. A common usage for order maximum is chemical compounds that are restricted in quantity for safety reasons.

These three order modifiers are commonly used together, but an item does not have to have an order minimum, maximum, and multiple at the same time. Many items' lot sizes only need to be defined by one of these order rules. The tool selected must match the needs of the item.

## Period of Supply (POS)

The most useful of the order sizing tools is the period of supply. This allows the planner to determine how many times each year an order should be placed, and the lot size adjusts dynamically to the demands from the top-level master schedule. If the period of supply is set to five, the order quantity will be calculated starting at the ordering point, and all requirements five periods into the future are added into the planned order quantity. If the periods are days, this would mean that the item would be ordered once per week. The advantage to this approach is that once the end of the defined horizon is reached, the end of the inventory is also reached. Like lot for lot, no leftover inventory remains in stock unless safety stock has been defined for the part. If safety stock has been defined, the inventory level will fall to that quantity at the end of the defined period horizon. This is not true of any of the other described lot size methods.

One way to choose how often the part should be ordered and therefore how many should be ordered at a time is to use the economic order quantity as a starting point. For example, if the economic order quantity for a part with annual sales of 5000 parts is 250 parts, this means that the planner is expected to order 5000/250 or 20 times per year. Given there are 240 average work days per year, the period of supply would be 12 days. Each time the need for ordering arises, the material planning system would look out the next 12 days and add together all the requirements into one planned order. Now the same part A used in the previous examples will be planned with a different order sizing rule. The planned orders shown in Table 7–7 are different in quantity and timing than the previous examples.

On average, the planner would expect to order this part 20 times each year. This process of relating the period of supply to the economic order quantity is called period order quantity (POQ).

**T A B L E   7–7**

Period of Supply=3

| Item ID: A  Lot size=POS(3), Low Lvl=0, OH=300  LT=1, Alloc=0, SS=150 | 1 | 2 | 3 | 4 | 5 | 6 | 7 | 8 |
|---|---|---|---|---|---|---|---|---|
| Master Schedule | 100 | 400 | 200 | 300 | 100 | 200 | 300 | 100 |
| Scheduled Receipts | 400 | | | | | | | |
| Projected on Hand | 600 | 200 | 550 | 250 | 150 | 550 | 250 | 150 |
| Planned Order Receipts | | | 550 | | | 600 | | |
| Planned Order Releases | | 550 | | | 600 | | | |

Period order quantity uses the strength of the economic order quantity while downplaying its disadvantages. The actual calculation and determination of the economic order quantity and the period order quantity are handled outside the traditional Material Requirements Planning system. The values are input into a single field in the item master that the system uses when calculating planned orders.

## SUMMARY

The answer to how much to order can vary widely based on the characteristics of the parts and the goals of the organizations. Understanding order sizing tools is essential to setting up the item master correctly. Accurate setup of the item master will benefit the planners by giving only real action messages, rather than some that amount to "noise." Lot sizing rules can dramatically reduce the number of planner messages while still achieving the company's overall inventory objectives. Regular review of lot sizing rules is recommended to ensure that the proper rule is being used.

While minimizing planner messages, lot size rules other than lot for lot and periods of supply have a way of building inventory.

MRP plans materials to be available when needed, in the amounts required to support the operation. Planners are responsible for reacting to the imbalances between the plan and the real world. Good creativity and problem-solving skills are needed for a planner to be successful. Understanding the underlying logic of the MRP explosion allows the planner to utilize the resources of the company the best way possible.

# 8

## ⑥ WORKING WITH THE TOOLS

## INTRODUCTION

When implementing an integrated planning and control system, the goal is to have suppliers deliver exactly what is needed, when needed, on all purchased parts. Manufacturing builds only what is required with no waste of resources, exactly on time. Sounds like a dream world, doesn't it? In fact, material requirement planning systems calculate the plan exactly this way. The requirement date is backed off by the estimated lead time, and all materials are planned to be available at the time of order release, not one day before or after.

Modern MRP systems allow filters on the planner's action messages so that the planner is not inundated with meaningless messages like rescheduling an order forward or back by a day. However, in some businesses that one day can be critical. The more inventories are reduced and the closer the facility gets to the final goal of zero inventory, the more that one day matters. However, most companies run with some pool of inventory. Recall that the functions of inventory include anticipation, fluctuation, lot size, cycle stock, hedge, and transportation. These are many good reasons to carry more inventory than the requirements only for immediate needs. Real-world situations, including setup times and lot charges, can be included as part of the normal planning process. The system must be set to accurately respond in a realistic way. Otherwise, the planner could easily begin to ignore the system output. Some basic tools allow the planner to manipulate the MRP-calculated internal schedule and ensure that the resulting plan is realistic and achievable.

## PLANNED ORDERS

Planned orders are replenishment orders created by the material requirement planning system in response to a part's requirement. These orders are changed, rescheduled, and deleted automatically by the system. At the appropriate time, a planner would examine the planned order, determine if sufficient materials and capacity existed to complete the order, and then would open the order and release it to the shop. Few MRP systems offer an automatic order release option since this examination of raw materials and capacity availability is a critical planning function not well delegated to the computer. For the management of the production area to be most effective, the planned order should have all its required components and sufficient capacity available. Opening orders with shortages is a sure way to begin an expediting function in the plant. This function adds no value but does add significant cost to the operation. Production personnel cannot be efficient if they must begin an order and set it aside. Quality and on-time delivery usually suffer as well. However, there are some environments where automatically opening work orders is possible and feasible. These businesses have a highly repetitive production environment with few exceptions or changes. Entrepreneurial (small) businesses tend to be in a highly variable make-to-order environment with many exceptions and changes—not a good environment for automatic order release.

If the business and manufacturing environment is stable enough that the release of orders can be automated, this automatic release feature can be very nice to have. Most entrepreneurial businesses do not have that level of stability in their material and capacity plans. Just the ability to release a work order without any part shortages can be a major accomplishment for the small plant. Changing demands from the customer cause frequent disruption of the material and capacity plans. The material requirements planning system provides the visibility of these changes and the impact on the operation. Once the order has been opened and released, MRP will not automatically adjust the order in any way.

The planners' exception messages are the communication from the computer system that the requirements and replenishments do not match. MRP will attempt to match the supply and demand for a part within the tolerance assigned in the system. A skilled planner will resolve these planner action messages at the lowest possible level of the bill of material so that the impact on the balance of the shop is minimized. Although rescheduling the customer order is a possible way to solve the problem of a mismatched supply and demand, it is the least desirable option. First, any flexibility internally must be explored before the customer is impacted. Only as a last resort should the customer's order be moved.

## FIRM PLANNED ORDERS

Sometimes a planner wants to schedule the capacity and materials for an order without opening the order. Releasing the order allocates the inventory and capacity. The planner merely wants to plan the requirements, not allocate them. Firm planned orders are one way to accomplish this goal. Firm planned orders are frequently used to establish a plan for some unique event, such as bringing a tool or machine down for maintenance. The planner desires to build inventory ahead of that event or to schedule a production window for other reasons. The firm planned order is frozen in quantity and timing, and the material requirement planning system will not move it. However, similar to released orders, MRP will send error messages to the planner when the timing of the replenishment order does not line up with the corresponding requirements.

Assume that there is a change in the customer's demand in Table 8–1. In Table 8–2, the demand in periods 5 and 6 both increase to 400. MRP will automatically plan order releases to match the increase in demands with replenishment orders.

The manufacturing planner knows that the production facility will run more efficiently if there is no shutdown between the orders beginning on week 5 and week 7. Usually manufacturing

**TABLE 8-1**

Original MRP Plan

| Item ID: A<br>Lot size=400, Low Lvl=0, OH=300<br>LT=1, Alloc=0, SS=150 | 1 | 2 | 3 | 4 | 5 | 6 | 7 | 8 |
|---|---|---|---|---|---|---|---|---|
| Customer Demand | 100 | 400 | 200 | 300 | 100 | 200 | 300 | 100 |
| Scheduled Receipts | 400 | | | | | | | |
| Projected on Hand | 600 | 200 | 400 | 500 | 400 | 200 | 300 | 200 |
| Planned Order Receipts | | | 400 | 400 | | | 400 | |
| Planned Order Releases | | 400 | 400 | | | 400 | | |

**TABLE 8-2**

After Demand Change

| Item ID: A<br>Lot size=400, Low Lvl=0, OH=300<br>LT=1, Alloc=0, SS=150 | 1 | 2 | 3 | 4 | 5 | 6 | 7 | 8 |
|---|---|---|---|---|---|---|---|---|
| Customer Demand | 100 | 400 | 200 | 300 | 400 | 400 | 300 | 100 |
| Scheduled Receipts | 400 | | | | | | | |
| Projected on Hand | 600 | 200 | 400 | 500 | 500 | 500 | 200 | 500 |
| Planned Order Receipts | | | 400 | 400 | 400 | 400 | | 400 |
| Planned Order Releases | | 400 | 400 | 400 | 400 | | 400 | |

**TABLE  8–3**

After Firm Planned Order

| Item ID: A<br>Lot size=400, Low Lvl=0, OH=300<br>LT=1, Alloc=0, SS=150 | 1 | 2 | 3 | 4 | 5 | 6 | 7 | 8 |
|---|---|---|---|---|---|---|---|---|
| Customer Demand | 100 | 400 | 200 | 300 | 400 | 400 | 300 | 100 |
| Scheduled Receipts | 400 | | | | | | | |
| Projected on Hand | 600 | 200 | 400 | 500 | 500 | 500 | 600 | 500 |
| Planned Order Receipts | | | 400 | 400 | 400 | 400 | 400 | |
| Planned Order Releases | | 400 | 400 | 400 | 400 | 400F | | |

facilities work better when they continually produce, not when they are shut down and started up. To take advantage of this manufacturing efficiency, the planner firm plans an order to begin in week 6. The result on the inventory is shown in Table 8–3.

Placing the firm planned order in period 6 increases inventory in period 7. This increase in inventory should be offset by the increased manufacturing efficiency gained by not stopping and starting production. These balancing decisions are the core of the manufacturing planner's job. If the order in period 6 was not firm planned, when MRP ran next, the order would be moved automatically out to period 7 again (Figure 8–2). Since the order is firm planned (denoted by the F), the MRP calculation will not move the order but will send a message to the planner that the order is a week early. Having the firm planned order reflect exactly what the intent is for the manufacturing production schedule, the planner can communicate to everyone the intended plan without releasing the order. Purchasing will know that materials are required to support the order beginning in period 6. Other manufactured parts required to build this part will also be planned to arrive when needed. The firm planned order is a simple tool with far-reaching impact. This method is commonly used for master scheduling at the end-item level. The master scheduler firm plans the replenishment work orders to optimize the use of capacity and to address any known material shortages. These top-level manufacturing orders then drive all the dependent demand to fulfill the plan. Rarely will the customer orders arrive such that the capacity and material plan are level. This is the job of the master scheduler. The firm planned order is a critical tool in the planner and scheduler's toolbox.

## RESOLVING PLANNER MESSAGES

Identification of the mismatch between requirements and replenishment is only the beginning of the story. Reacting to and resolving each planner message while maintaining a realistic schedule is the core responsibility of the planner. The actions and procedures usually taken by the planner are described for each of the following messages.

### Release Purchase Order

The planner must consider the overall requirements for the part and determine a realistic schedule. MRP provides the visibility of many future requirements provided that the master schedule has been input for a sufficient time horizon into the future. Blanket orders covering more than one replenishment are possible with this visibility. This feature is one reason that companies using MRP are more competitive in their material purchasing. This forward visibility allows the customer to plan more effectively and provides a realistic plan to the supplier. The realistic plan allows the supplier to plan more effectively and will save the customer money. Suppliers are usually willing to provide large quantity discounts for blanket orders placed with multiple shipments. This increased visibility provides an opportunity for the supplier to optimize its production schedules and level load its capacity. Shorter lead time orders can then be worked around this precommitted schedule of known requirements. This openness and sharing of MRP information is a success strategy for supplier partnerships. Some companies allow suppliers to look directly at the MRP reports for their end-item parts they make for the customer supplying the report. These action reports within a certain time horizon are the authorization for the supplier to begin its manufacturing process. Agreements are made between the customer and supplier concerning the length of the time horizon that is authorized. Procurement of long lead time materials can be authorized for an additional length of time. Visibility in addition to that horizon is information only for the supplier used to communicate overall expected production levels.

## Release Manufacturing Order

Unlike the purchase order that can be released for many deliveries of the same part, manufacturing orders are released one delivery at a time. Blanket orders cannot be issued to the shop. Unique orders are released for each delivery. The first step of releasing a manufacturing order should be to check components to ensure that all are available. An example of this function is shown in Figure 8–1. For this product and work order quantity, three of the four components required for the product have sufficient quantities in inventory to satisfy the demand for the work order. Only one part, the cork grip, is short. The current inventory status is –50! Two flags go up in this situation. First, since the inventory is negative, a physical count of parts is definitely warranted. During this count, the underlying issue that caused the inventory to go negative must be addressed. Usually an incoming lot of material was not transacted to the system. The second flag that goes up is not to release the order until the inventory has been verified. The order can be released if sufficient quantities (25) are available.

To optimize the flow in the production shop, the order should not be released if any of the components are short. Some production managers believe that working on partial work orders is the only way that the shop can keep busy and satisfy the customer demands. The reality is that releasing work to the production area without all the parts causes nonvalue-added time to be spent

**F I G U R E   8–1**

Check Components

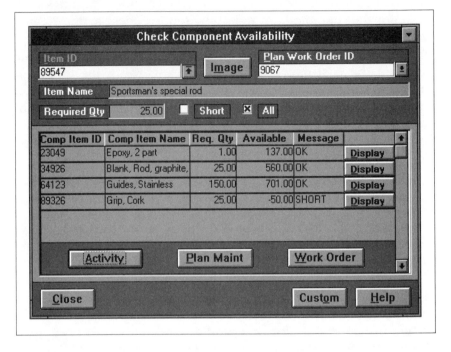

matching late arriving parts for shortages with the correct work order. Usually in the process of waiting for shortage parts to arrive, the other parts have disappeared. The lack of complete parts for the production process causes the direct labor personnel to be less efficient, and the quality usually suffers. The belief behind releasing partial orders to the shop is that manufacturing can get started and can put the missing parts in at the last minute and make the shipment on time. Real-world experience shows that the opposite is true. Releasing work orders with shortages usually means that less work is accomplished, and the overall lack of discipline results in less revenue completed and shipped. Discipline is a key part of making any system work, whether it is manual or computerized. Not releasing orders that are short parts is an important discipline.

## Reschedule Orders

The message to reschedule looks like the easiest to accomplish. If only the key strokes required to accomplish the changes were considered, that statement would be true. However, rescheduling orders can be a tricky business. Most companies have a tolerance for the arrival of parts, both early and late. Rescheduling within these tolerances does not add value. Many modern MRP systems provide a function to filter planner messages for this tolerance. This significantly reduces the number of planner messages and makes the planner messages more realistic. The planner must clearly understand the strategic goals of the business with respect to sensitivity for rescheduling. The tolerances set for the message analysis must be consistent with the overall customer service goals. The lower the inventory level becomes, the more critical the rescheduling becomes. A plant that delivers to its customer on a daily basis must be more concerned with a one-day variance between needed and scheduled dates than a plant that schedules in weekly time buckets.

## PLANNER MESSAGE STRATEGY

A key success strategy for the company is to have the planner able to react quickly to important situations. An expected benefit of an implementation is that more parts can be planned and managed by the same number of people. This allows the company to grow without increasing overhead expense. The overhead cost per part declines and the plant is more profitable. This in turn hopefully fuels additional growth and even more increased profitability. Unfortunately, when implementing an automated MRP system, the most overwhelming thing is the quantity of planner messages after the first MRP run. The number of planner messages can make even the most seasoned professional wince. Some wonder how they will ever be able to get everything under control. Unfortunately, there is no classroom where planners can go and learn the trade of planning.

When implementing an MRP system, one of the first steps is overall top-level education. The student learns the theory on how MRP systems work to help manage a business by providing improved information and visibility. After the top-level education is complete, system-specific training is done. Here the student learns how to push the buttons on the keyboard to make the computer software work. Between the theory and the skills there is a big gap. Nowhere is application skill taught. How do we take this new computer software and use it to manage *our* business? What is it that I want the computer software to do? System training taught what keys to push—but what activities do I want to accomplish? What are the desired business objectives? How do I fit all these different tools to my situation? What goes first? These and a million other questions must be answered during the implementation. The theory of planner messages is common sense. There is an imbalance between the plan and the actual tactics. However, this imbalance can lead to a quantity of messages that is larger than can be addressed in a timely fashion. The following sections describe some tools that will help even the most experienced planner through the maze of planner messages.

## Prioritize Using Low-Level Codes

When first looking at the material plan, work down the planning tree just as MRP did the planning. Work all the planner messages for low-level code 0 items first before moving on to level 1. Parent items should be worked before their components. The most common error made by planners is working exception messages in item-number sequence. Frequently a change will be made on a parent after the component level item has been balanced. Now the planner must rebalance all the associated components again, creating even more work for the planner. This rebalancing becomes a vicious circle until the planner just gives up.

Planners often work messages in the order the system displays them, even though it may not be the most effective way. Computer software was written by programmers, not planners. Sorting messages by part number makes sense to a programmer. There could not be a worse situation for a planner. Fortunately, new systems today are more flexible for reporting. Storing data in tables accessible with a simple report writing tool is common for most systems. Developing a different sort criteria for parts requiring attention is no longer an impossible dream. The most efficient way to work planner messages is low-level code order. Depending on the system used, a net change MRP run may be needed between levels to drive the revised requirements to the next level. This is a small price to pay to be significantly more efficient. Low-level code prioritization prevents entering an infinite loop of planner messages. Each part can be worked only once in a very efficient manner, the same way the computer works.

## Bottom-Up Replanning

When material problems arise, and they will, resolve the issue as low as possible in the bill of material. For example, in Table 8–4, the planned order release for period 2 cannot be accomplished due to a material shortage on a component. Inventory of the component is sufficient to build only 300 of the parent part. The delivery from the supplier is expected in period 3. What to do? Should the planned order be moved to period 3 or should a partial order be released? Another alternative is to release the order in period

### T A B L E   8–4

Shortage Situation

**Item ID: A**
Lot size=400, Low Lvl=0, OH=300
LT=1, Alloc=0, SS=150

| | 1 | 2 | 3 | 4 | 5 | 6 | 7 | 8 |
|---|---|---|---|---|---|---|---|---|
| Customer Demand | 100 | 400 | 200 | 300 | 100 | 200 | 300 | 100 |
| Scheduled Receipts | 400 | | | | | | | |
| Projected on Hand | 600 | 200 | 400 | 500 | 400 | 200 | 300 | 200 |
| Planned Order Receipts | | | 400 | 400 | | | 400 | |
| Planned Order Releases | | 400 | 400 | | | 400 | | |

2 with the shortage and set the part of the order with the shortage aside until the shipment arrives

The last alternative is the worst. Regardless of when the part is used in the manufacturing process, releasing work to the shop floor with a part's shortage causes many problems that were described earlier. Examining the other two alternatives gives these possible results: If the order release was moved to period 3, the projected on hand would fall to zero. The forecasted customer demand is satisfied, but safety stock was defined for this part for presumably a good reason. In addition, moving the release of this order to period 3 doubles the demand for that period. Sufficient capacity becomes a concern. Doubling output in one period can be an issue for many facilities.

The last option is to release the order for less than the fixed order quantity. Table 8–5 shows the impact. Safety stock is preserved for the part. Due to the decrease in the order size, the order that was originally scheduled for period 6 has been moved to period 5. An additional order is planned for period 7. Adding the

TABLE 8–5

Possible Resolution

**Item ID: A**
Lot size=400, Low Lvl=0, OH=300
LT=1, Alloc=0, SS=150

|  | 1 | 2 | 3 | 4 | 5 | 6 | 7 | 8 |
|---|---|---|---|---|---|---|---|---|
| Customer Demand | 100 | 400 | 200 | 300 | 100 | 200 | 300 | 100 |
| Scheduled Receipts | 400 | | | | | | | |
| Projected on Hand | 600 | 200 | 300 | 400 | 300 | 500 | 200 | 500 |
| Planned Order Receipts | | | 300 | 400 | | 400 | | 400 |
| Planned Order Releases | | | 300 | 400 | | 400 | | 400 |

100 that were reduced from the period 2 release to the period 3 will prevent these two planning changes. When selecting which alternative to use, keep in mind the desire to minimize the disruption in the balance of the system. This may entail making less than the calculated optimal order quantity, but what is really important is to deliver the product to the customer on the promised date. Splitting lots and building a smaller order is a small price to pay. Again, the decision is made from an overall business consideration. This process is called bottom-up replanning.

When replanning and resolving problems, orders do not have to be released. Using a firm planned order can communicate the intended plan to the rest of the organization. This visibility communicates the real need date for the components. Another planner could be expediting parts at increased cost to support production only to find that production is delayed due to another shortage. Keeping the material plan valid provides this essential communication. Many times one problem solved can relieve other problems or save expedite costs of related component items. This is the motivation behind keeping the system information up to date and accurate.

## Order Release Discipline

This recommendation has been discussed in other areas but bears repeating here. Release work orders when all the parts and capacity are available and the timing is right. In other words, release no work order before its time or when it is short. This may seem impossible since many plants have fallen into the practice of releasing work orders so that production can get started on them even though they are still missing parts. The purpose is to keep the shop busy or the belief is that shipments will not be made unless the process is continued. Let's face it: the plant is not going to ship anything that is still short parts. Why get into this very bad habit? Like extended overtime, releasing work orders short parts can be a tough habit to break. Providing production the opportunity to start on the order and put it aside usually provides an excellent opportunity for that order (or individual parts in the other) to get lost. This practice increases the labor requirement for the finished parts and usually has a negative impact on quality, efficiency, and locating parts. Relieving shortages to these kits entails significant work that consumes many hours better spent getting it right the first time. When all the negative consequences are considered, this really is a bad deal. Short orders is a very difficult habit to break, but breaking the habit is an important part of the discipline required for MRP and any other advanced tool like Just-In-Time manufacturing.

## Trust Your Data

Trust your data. Insist on discipline and accountability. Rechecking the data (yours and other users) and other information from the system takes a significant amount of time and effort. These efforts only begin to scratch the surface of data inaccuracy. The number one reason that MRP implementations fail is due to data inaccuracy. Rechecking data on a spot check random basis will not help. Systemwide process controls, such as cycle counting and bill of material validation, must be in place to ensure record accuracy. A strange phenomenon happens once the assumption is made that the data are accurate and decisions are made based on that information. Data accuracy usually improves. The informal system is no longer used as a crutch. This commitment to use the formal system focuses everyone's efforts on making the information useable. Resources are not available to keep two systems running. Pick which one to use and focus on only one. If the attempt is made to use both the old and new system, there is one guaranteed result—they will both be wrong.

## Address Underlying Issues

Do not merely delete planner messages and hope they will go away. Many planners delete planner messages from the screen and then are upset when they come back after the next planning run. Ignoring or deleting them does not make them go away. Only addressing the underlying causes of the message will make the message go away. The message is there for a reason. If you do not like the message, change the reason. This may mean a correction to a bill of material, an adjustment to a master schedule, an order sizing rule change, lead time adjustment, or other inventory record update. The key behind this tool is to understand why the system has calculated what it has. Fixing the issue eliminates the message for good and gives better information to the planner and other users of the system. Once planner messages are ignored, the whole use of the system deteriorates quickly. Remember that MRP is really quite simple. The system looks at what you need, compares it to what you have, and tells you what to go get and when. If the "what you need to go get" is wrong, then there probably is a problem with the "what you have" or the "what you need." Fixing the root cause for one part fixes the problem for all the other related components.

## SUMMARY

Once realistic material plans have been made for each time period, purchasing and the shop floor can go to work. Planner messages are the communication from the system that supply and demand are not in alignment. MRP can perform its calculations with any schedule, any inventory, and any bill of material. Planner messages are based on these calculations. The quality of the information from the user determines how realistic and useable the plan will be. Using tools like firm planned orders and lot quantity modifiers helps deliver a realistic, workable plan to the users of the system. The five planner strategies will help focus planning activities on the appropriate parts to address the underlying issues. The worst possible condition is to start ignoring situations to which the computer is alerting you. This is a very easy habit to develop and is very dangerous because soon messages that should have been responded to are ignored. At this point the formal system starts to deteriorate and the communication among everyone in the organization begins to deteriorate. The informal system is always waiting to step back in. If the system is generating messages that are meaningless, the underlying condition creating those messages must be addressed and rectified; otherwise the messages will continue (and be ignored), and the slide back towards the informal system has begun. Remember that you have been there and done that before. Do you really want to go back?

# 9

⑥ CAPACITY
REQUIREMENTS
PLANNING

## INTRODUCTION

Even if materials are well planned and available, they cannot be converted to finished goods without adequate capacity. Additional planning is required to determine the availability and need of these critical resources. To aid in the capacity planning process, a tool known as capacity requirements planning (CRP) was developed. Capacity requirements planning is defined in the 8th edition of the APICS dictionary as:

> The function of establishing, measuring, and adjusting limits or levels of capacity. The term "capacity requirements planning" (CRP) in this context refers to the process of determining in detail the amount of labor and machine resources required to accomplish the tasks of production. Open shop orders and planned orders in the MRP system are input to CRP. These orders are translated through the use of part routings and time standards into hours of work by work center by time period. Even though rough-cut capacity planning may indicate that sufficient capacity exists to execute the Master Production Schedule, CRP may show that capacity is insufficient during specific time periods.

Capacity requirements planning follows exactly the same logic as materials requirements planning and plans the amount of critical resources needed to carry out the master production schedule. These resources can be labor-hours, machine-hours, cash, or any other constraint to the process. Capacity requirements planning answers the question, How much resource is required and when is it required? Critical resources can be identified by asking the question, What must be added to increase output? Becoming locked into thinking about capacity in terms of workers or machine time is easy. However, in the small company, the bottleneck critical resource may not be either of these two factors, but it could be space or cash. The first step in planning detailed capacity is to define the resource bottleneck. This is usually easy to spot. The piles of work in process in front of the resource bottleneck are a sure giveaway. If the process is not completed at this resource, upstream and downstream operation scheduling really does not matter. CRP can monitor this bottleneck and other near-bottlenecks closely and provide information about the load projected into the future. Since CRP can track many resources simultaneously, this process will prevent planning capacity for resources that do not affect output and possibly miss resources that are critical to increased output.

## LEVELS OF CAPACITY PLANNING

Capacity planning should occur at many levels. During the production planning process, a check is made against available long lead resources like facilities, large capital equipment, and total headcount to ensure that the production plan is reasonable. When this plan is further broken down into the master production schedule, another validation of capacity is done to ensure that the master production schedule is achievable. These capacity requirements are in finer detail and include shorter horizon items like major department capacity and overall shift requirements. Further detail of the capacity planning process is done after material requirements planning to ensure that individual resources are not overloaded and to provide near-term visibility of future needs for critical resources. This detailed capacity planning process is called capacity requirements planning. The different levels of capacity planning do not directly drive each other as do the priority plans. In priority planning, the production plan drives the master schedule, and the master schedule in turn drives the material plan. The production plan is a total of the more detailed master production schedule. MRP is directly linked back to the MPS. In capacity planning, the resources planned are calculated from each level of the priority plan, not from the higher-level resource plan. The capacity plan validates each level of priority planning. Validating the priority plan with a capacity check closes the planning loop and increases the chances for success in achieving the overall business plan.

Entrepreneurial businesses are great at making big plans but can fall short of achieving them because the resources required are underestimated or not considered at all. Unfortunately, many small companies ignore this vital tool of planning because they believe they can manage without it. Remember, your father always told you that the job is easier when you use the right tool for the right job, and you can spend each dollar only once. In manufacturing, the advice is no different. In earlier chapters, resource planning and rough-cut capacity planning were discussed. Now, let's turn our attention to the most detailed capacity plan that closes the loop to the execution of the material priority plan.

## USING CAPACITY PLANNING

Recall from the MRP discussion that all materials are calculated to be available at the start of the lead time for the replenishment order. MRP takes the estimated lead time from the item master file and schedules all material to be available at the time of order release. However, capacity is consumed at different times in different places as the order moves through the shop. Shop orders can be scheduled backward from the desired completion date or forward from an identified start date.

**Example    Backward Scheduling—Order Due for Completion at the End of Day 12**
According to backward scheduling logic, the order would be scheduled to start at the beginning of day 3. Provided the lead

time in the item master is 9 days or longer, the materials will
be scheduled in advance of the expected order start.

```
1  2   3     4      5       6    7      8    9      10      11  12

      setup A      run A        queue              setup B    run B
      +_____+_____+_____+_____+_____+
```

If the lead time is less than 9 days, say, 5 days, the order would
be scheduled to start before the materials would be scheduled to
be available.

**Example    Forward Schedule—Order to Begin at the Start
of Day 1**

```
1      2     3      4      5      6   7    8    9      10     11    12

setup A      run A        queue           setup B    run B
+_____+_____+_____+_____+_____+
```

Given this forward schedule, the order should be completed at the
beginning of day 11. The utilization of resource is very different
from the backward scheduled order. Resource A would be needed
in days 1 through 4 for the forward scheduled order and would
be needed in days 3 through 6 for the backward scheduled order.
Resource B is needed between day 7 and 11 for the forward scheduled order and day 9 through 12 for the backward scheduled
order. Just the choice of scheduling a single order can result in a
very different load profile.

The expected total cumulative lead time in this detailed
capacity planning has little chance of equaling the estimated lead
time from the item master. The cumulative lead time is the total
of the setup time, run time, and move and queue times. Since the
run time is variable based on the size of the lot, the total cumulative lead time changes as the lot size changes. Materials are
planned based on the fixed lead time in the item master. Capacity is planned based on the desired order scheduling rule to determine how much capacity is needed, at what location, and when.

The capacity plan translates into dispatch lists, which are
detailed schedules by day for the shop floor. Dispatch lists are used
by the shop floor to determine what to work on next and what
can be expected in the future. In the examples used previously,
work area A would have had the order on its dispatch list starting day 3 for the backward scheduled scenario and day 1 for the
forward scheduled order. The completion date on the dispatch
list is day 6 for the backward scheduled order and day 4 for the

forward scheduled order. Other orders would be scheduled in a similar fashion to provide complete visibility of load for the work area. More important than communicating what to work on next is the forward visibility of future demand for critical resources. This allows an opportunity to be proactive in solving imbalances. Just like planning material, capacity use does not have to be forecast. CRP allows the future capacity plan to be calculated, giving a more accurate and more reliable plan. The real value is knowing that a problem is going to arise *before* it becomes a crisis. A plan can then be formulated to resolve the problem before it goes to the shop floor.

## REQUIREMENTS FOR CRP

MRP has some very simple system requirements and, similarly, so does CRP. The CRP requirements follow.

### Units of Capacity

This is similar to the unit of measure for the item master. The most commonly used unit of measure for planning capacity is hours. This can be machine-hours or people-hours. Another unit of capacity that is critical for entrepreneurial business is dollars. If there is a large outlay of financial resources during the manufacturing process, if possible, that outlay needs to occur close to the end of the process. Projecting a detailed, day-by-day cash flow is required in many entrepreneurial businesses. Another unit of capacity more commonly used to validate the master schedule and production plan is square feet. This capacity measure can also be used on a more detailed level to calculate storage area or pallet positions required. If space is a critical constraint, close planning of this resource may be required. The capacity unit of measure answers the question, What do we need to add to increase output?

Tooling needed for the production process can be planned as part of the capacity plan by treating it as another work center. The unit of measure usually is hours. Another method for planning tooling is to treat it like a component item on the bill of material with a certain amount of hours "in stock" that are consumed as the tool is used. This process allows the calibration, overhaul, or replacement of a tool to be planned into the future based on actual, scheduled utilization. Once again, the integration of MRP and CRP allows the calculation of these events rather than having to forecast them (and be wrong).

## Routings

Routings are the sequential steps that the raw materials and other parts must follow to be completed. Other commonly used names for routings are bill of operations, instruction sheet, manufacturing data sheet, operation chart, operation list, operation sheet, route sheet, and routing sheet. The most difficult step in developing routings is to make the choice between a routing step or bill of material level. If the semifinished state will be stocked or sold or if detailed data collection is desired, a level in the bill of material is required. This means that the order must be closed and received to inventory at this level to be issued on the next higher assembly. The requirement for this transaction does not mean that the part must move to a storeroom. A transaction must take place completing one work order before issuing the part onto another order. These transactions can take place without the part moving. If the semifinished state is temporary and is moved directly to the next operation within a short period of time, a routing step is all that is required.

As companies reduce lead time and decrease the levels in the bills of material, steps in the routing are added. The parts do not go into and out of inventory. Instead, they stay on the shop floor until totally completed and are ready to go to the customer. Figure 9–1 is a sample of a routing for a part that travels through three works areas—assembly, drilling, and packaging. Detailed information is stored in the routing concerning the amount of time schedule for setup, machine-hours, and labor-hours Additional reference information is included about the designated machine and any special tool kit or CNC tape required to run the parts. The routing describes the path the manufactured part will follow to completion.

### Cellular Manufacturing Routings
Implementing cellular manufacturing simplifies the routings by eliminating all the intermediate steps and routes the part into the

FIGURE   9-1

Routing

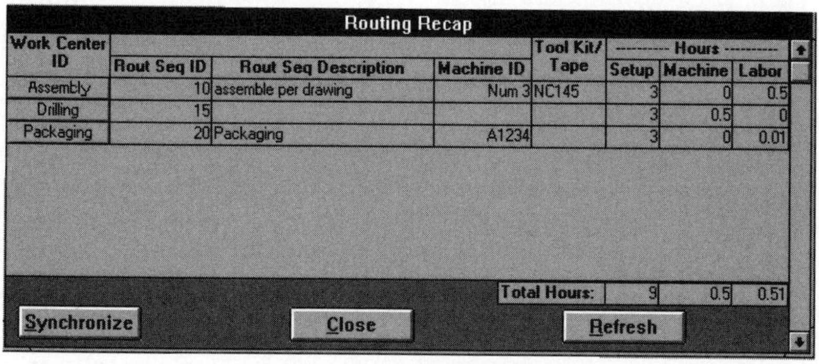

| Work Center ID | Rout Seq ID | Rout Seq Description | Machine ID | Tool Kit/ Tape | Setup | Machine | Labor |
|---|---|---|---|---|---|---|---|
| | | | | | ------ Hours ------ | | |
| Assembly | 10 | assemble per drawing | Num 3 | NC145 | 3 | 0 | 0.5 |
| Drilling | 15 | | | | 3 | 0.5 | 0 |
| Packaging | 20 | Packaging | A1234 | | 3 | 0 | 0.01 |
| | | | | Total Hours: | 9 | 0.5 | 0.51 |

Synchronize        Close        Refresh

cell as a single work center rather than a series of individual operations. A cell is a collection of dissimilar machines that perform all the functions required to complete the part. To change from the traditional bill of material structure to these "flattened" bills, phantom parts are used. Phantom parts (make-on-assembly) have no lead time and are expected to have no inventory. Usually the designation is made in the item master that the part is considered a phantom. Using phantoms simplifies the flattening of a deep bill of material because the bill does not need to be restructured. Only a simple change to the item master is needed to reflect the phantom status. The bill of material continues to match the drawing tree.

Special care must be taken when developing routings to determine the most commonly used sequence and work areas to complete the parts. Many modern systems allow the input of alternate routings, but realistically keeping one set of routings accurate is a big enough task for most companies. No CRP system is intelligent enough to reroute a part through the alternate routing. That is the job of the skilled planner. The defined routing in the computer should be the most likely sequence of where the work will be accomplished and how long each operation is expected to take.

## Schedule

The schedule of orders used as the input to CRP is a direct output of the material requirements planning (MRP) process. Released and planned orders can be used to provide future visibility of capacity needs. If only released orders are used, the load pattern falls off quickly and gives a false picture of the future need for resources. See Figure 9–2.

If the actual capacity for this area was 60 hours, the manager could come to the incorrect conclusion that a production window opened up to complete the past due work beginning in period 5. Using all orders, released and planned, allows the analyst or supervisor to have a more complete picture of the need for capacity. Only considering released orders can cause incorrect conclusions to be drawn about the need for capacity in the future. A realistic picture of capacity demands into the future is given when both types of orders are considered. Looking at the

**FIGURE 9–2**

Released Orders Only

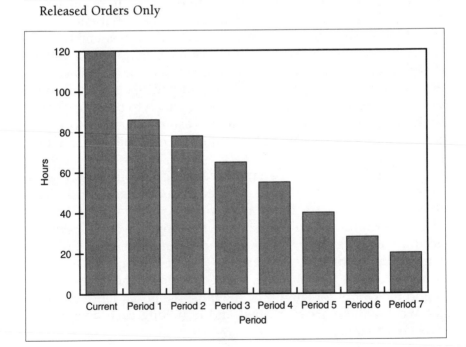

total picture, we see that if the capacity of the area is demonstrated to be 60 hours, the realization is obvious in Figure 9–3 that this area is in a significant overload position. There is no conceivable way to complete the work expected in the area. In addition, having planned work still in the current period begs the question, Why? Normally the work in the current period should be released and in work already. For this work area, there are only two choices. Either capacity must be increased or load must be decreased. The other option is a combination of the first two choices, increasing some capacity and decreasing some load. Ignoring this situation will not make it go away. The guarantee is that it will only get worse.

**F I G U R E   9–3**

Planned and Released Orders

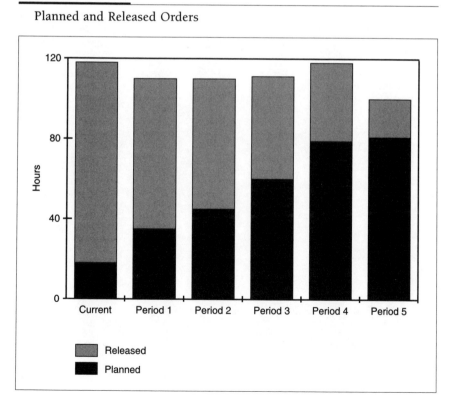

## Shop Calendar

The shop calendar defines what days the shop will work. The shop calendar is also known as the manufacturing calendar or M-day calendar. The benefit of having a shop calendar is that only realistic shop days will be used in the calculation of schedules. If there is a holiday inside the lead time, an extra calendar day is required to complete the order. A shop calendar gives a more accurate picture of expected completion dates since the non-working days are removed from the picture. A core requirement to implement capacity requirements planning is the definition of the shop calendar. This is usually done in the administrative function of the system. Figure 9–4 is an example of how a shop calendar is defined.

This calendar shows that the weekends, Saturday and Sunday, are not working days. In addition, December 25, Christmas, has also been identified as a nonworking day. Work can be scheduled more accurately when only working days are considered.

**FIGURE  9–4**

Shop Calendar

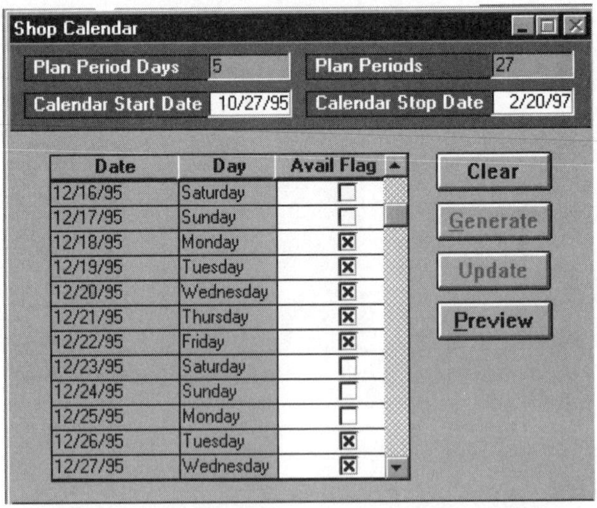

Shop Calendar

| Date | Day | Avail Flag |
|------|-----|------------|
| 12/16/95 | Saturday | ☐ |
| 12/17/95 | Sunday | ☐ |
| 12/18/95 | Monday | ☒ |
| 12/19/95 | Tuesday | ☒ |
| 12/20/95 | Wednesday | ☒ |
| 12/21/95 | Thursday | ☒ |
| 12/22/95 | Friday | ☒ |
| 12/23/95 | Saturday | ☐ |
| 12/24/95 | Sunday | ☐ |
| 12/25/95 | Monday | ☐ |
| 12/26/95 | Tuesday | ☒ |
| 12/27/95 | Wednesday | ☒ |

Plan Period Days 5    Plan Periods 27
Calendar Start Date 10/27/95    Calendar Stop Date 2/20/97

Clear   Generate   Update   Preview

## CAPACITY MANAGEMENT MEASURES

### Available Capacity

Available capacity is the level of resources on hand to fill the demand. Unlike inventory, available capacity cannot be carried from one period to the next. Once the day is gone, the amount of capacity available for the day is gone also. Understanding this phenomenon is very difficult for some managers. The production schedule should contain no past-due work orders because there is no past-due capacity. Using past-due dates in an attempt to drive priority is the first step on the road back to using the old informal system. A key measure of the effectiveness of the master schedule is how much past-due capacity is planned. Determining available time is accomplished by identifying the number of shifts the resource will be available each day and how much that resource can be utilized.

Figure 9–5 shows the expected capacity daily for the final assembly work area. At the current time no work is loaded against this available capacity.

**FIGURE   9–5**

Work Center Capacity Definition

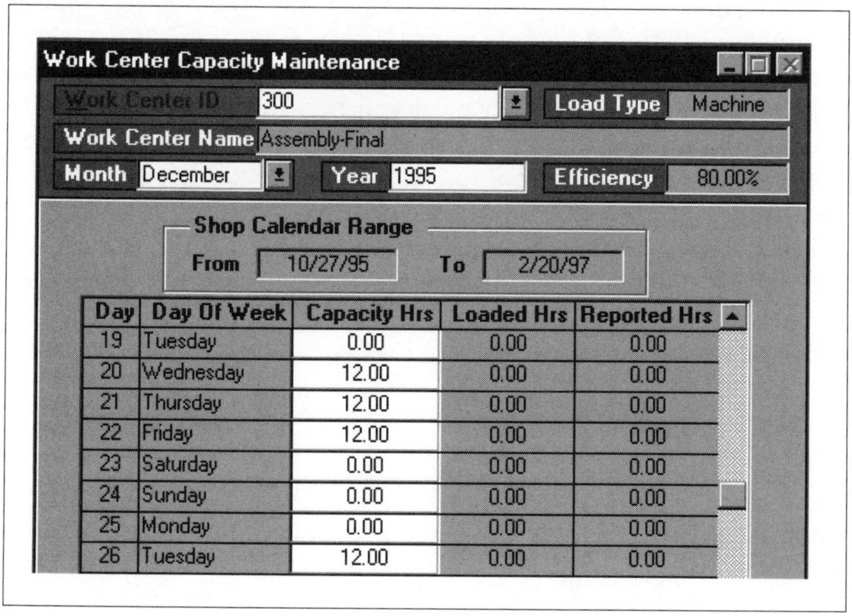

| Work Center Capacity Maintenance | | | | _ □ × |
|---|---|---|---|---|
| Work Center ID | 300 | ⭥ | Load Type | Machine |
| Work Center Name | Assembly-Final | | | |
| Month | December ⭥ | Year 1995 | Efficiency | 80.00% |

**Shop Calendar Range**

From [ 10/27/95 ]   To [ 2/20/97 ]

| Day | Day Of Week | Capacity Hrs | Loaded Hrs | Reported Hrs ▲ |
|---|---|---|---|---|
| 19 | Tuesday | 0.00 | 0.00 | 0.00 |
| 20 | Wednesday | 12.00 | 0.00 | 0.00 |
| 21 | Thursday | 12.00 | 0.00 | 0.00 |
| 22 | Friday | 12.00 | 0.00 | 0.00 |
| 23 | Saturday | 0.00 | 0.00 | 0.00 |
| 24 | Sunday | 0.00 | 0.00 | 0.00 |
| 25 | Monday | 0.00 | 0.00 | 0.00 |
| 26 | Tuesday | 12.00 | 0.00 | 0.00 |

## Utilization Factor

The utilization factor is usually expressed as a percentage between 0 and 100 percent. This is the percentage of time the resource is expected to run compared to the total time it is available. For example, if an NC machine is available two eight-hour shifts per day but the machine does not run unattended, the utilization of the machine would be reduced by the time for breaks and lunches (assume a total of two hours each day). The utilization factor of the NC machine would then be:

14 planned use hrs. / 16 total available hrs. = 87.5% utilization factor

Planning to utilize any resource 100 percent of its available time is a certain plan for failure. Every resource requires a certain amount of time for repair, maintenance, and rest. Scheduled preventive maintenance is not included in the utilization number. This activity is planned just like any other work order to use the resource. If the monthly preventive maintenance takes eight hours (all at one time), it makes little sense to schedule reduced utilization of 15 minutes per day. The better solution is to schedule an order that takes eight hours of capacity from the machine in one block.

In a make-to-order company, utilization is sometimes placed at conservatively low levels to provide a bank of safety capacity. This can be used to react to less than full lead time orders. These orders tend to have a higher price (higher profit) associated with them, and being able to react successfully to them can be a competitive strategy for the company. If the capacity is not used for these last-minute orders, usually enough backlog exists on the shop floor to consume the available capacity. The "utilization factor" is used for planning future capacity requirements and is different from the "utilization" calculation many people use to express what percentage of the payroll time was actually spent in productive activities.

## Efficiency

Efficiency is one of the most abused measures in manufacturing. Many companies use efficiency as a measure for people and their performance. In reality, efficiency is the measure of how well the standard times were established for each routing step. Efficiency is expressed as a percentage. If the actual time required to complete a routing step is less than the estimate, the efficiency is greater than 100 percent. If the actual time required to complete a routing step is more than the estimate, the efficiency is less than 100 percent.

The more that humans are involved in a process, the greater the variability of the efficiency. People vary one to another on how quickly they can complete a job. People vary day to day as to how quickly they can complete a job. Adding to this normal variability, learning curves come into play for tasks that are repeated. People performing a repetitive task get quicker as they perform more repetitions. As the process becomes more automated, the efficiency is less variable, and more accurate routing times can be established. Efficiency factors are like a coarse tuning knob for routings. Rather than changing the amount of hours in each routing step, application of an efficiency factor to the work center accomplishes a mass change very quickly. A key point to consider is that efficiency is not a performance measure of people. Efficiency is only a measure of the accuracy of the hour's estimate made in the routing. Many different factors can make a difference in the performance of the work area.

## Rated Capacity

Rated capacity is calculated by multiplying the planned daily capacity at the work center by the utilization factor by the efficiency factor.

### Example

One machine working one shift equals eight hours available. If that machine has a utilization factor of 85 percent and efficiency of 80 percent, the rated capacity is 5.44 hours ($8 \times .85 \times .8$). This result is an estimate of the capacity for the work center for each day.

Since rated capacity is a calculated number, there is an illusion of accuracy because of the appearance of numbers to the right of the decimal point. When using the information from a capacity planning system, also consider the underlying data supporting the information. An easy trap to fall into is that available capacity can be predicted accurately because a formula is used to calculate the number. One of the most exciting and frustrating parts of managing a plant is determining what the available capacity will be for the current day. People do not show up reliably for work. After reporting to work, people can leave suddenly. Day-to-day variations can be noticed in a worker's output. This illusion of accuracy and the inability to determine routing times exactly creates an unstable base on which to use finite scheduling.

## SCHEDULING OPTIONS

Once an estimate has been made of available capacity, orders can be scheduled into position for completion in a variety of ways.

### Backward Scheduling

The traditional method of scheduling the shop floor is to identify the desired completion date and then back up to the required start date. Capacity requirements planning backs through all the steps required to complete the order (the routing) and determines the start day for the order. The factors considered are the setup time, run time, move days, and queue days. The order these happen in is queue, setup, run, and move for each step in the routing. Therefore, when the backward scheduling is done, the last step of the routing is scheduled first by reversing the timing through move, run, setup, and queue to determine a start day. This start day is then used as the previous operation completion day, and the process is repeated until the start date of the first operation is determined.

### Forward Scheduling

Many times the customer will call and want to know, What is the earliest I can get this order? Traditional MRP only schedules in a backward manner given a desired completion date. This scheduling method does not help answer the customer's question.

Fortunately, newer systems allow the option of also scheduling forward given a start date. The scheduling logic is the same as backward scheduling where the order is progressively scheduled forwards through the planned queue, setup, run, and move time for each step in the process routing. The result is the soonest the order can be completed given normal lead time for each routing step. Often 80 to 90 percent of the total cumulative lead time comes from queue time, where no productive effort is being added to the order. Removal of this non-value-added time can dramatically reduce the overall elapsed time an order takes to complete. This is demonstrated on a daily basis when rush orders are expedited through the shop or at the end of the month when revenue targets are being pursued.

## Infinite Loading

The biggest criticism lately of MRP systems is that they are capacity insensitive. The netting and scheduling logic will schedule an order for completion regardless of the availability of capacity. One of the assumptions of MRP is that all input data are accurate and up to date. This includes the master production schedule (MPS). For the MPS to be realistic and accurate, the expected load must be compared to planned capacity. The planner is required to level load the shop and typically watches critical work centers for overload. Fewer routing steps and lower work in process make this job easier and more straightforward. This potential overall situation due to an unrealistic MPS has existed since MRP systems were originally developed. The main job of the planner was to resolve the resource conflicts and smooth the loading of the shop. Virtually every job shop has a bottleneck operation that can be easily identified by the pile of work waiting to be run. When this bottleneck is properly managed, the flow through the balance of the plant is usually very smooth. Figure 9–6 is an evample of an overloaded work center. The priority plan must be changed to better balance the capacity and the load. The drastic fluctuation between overload and underload is an unworkable condition for any facility. An effective planner will find a way to better balance the load and capacity.

**FIGURE   9–6**

Load versus Capacity

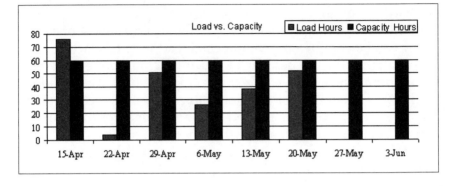

## Input/Output Control

Input/output control is a straightforward way to handle the bottleneck situation. Orders are released only for the quantity of work that has been completed through the bottleneck. Process improvement is focused on this bottleneck to reduce the amount of time required. Buffering this work center with some backlog of work ensures that it will not run out of work and therefore adversely impact the entire output of the plant. A sufficient buffer is needed to guard against running out of work, but not so much that additional lead time is created. This buffer is planned by defining queue for a work center. This queue time is scheduled into the sequential process for the job and becomes part of the standard flow. The work center can then expect to have that amount of planned queue waiting for processing. The actual amount of queue will depend on the reliability of the processes and the feasibility of the schedule. Figure 9–7 shows an example of the infinite loading process characteristic of traditional MRP systems. The current situation in the drilling department is sure to cause late orders in the plant.

## Finite Loading

The answer to the traditional capacity insensitivity of MRP and CRP is finite loading. This loading method will never exceed the

**FIGURE   9–7**

Infinite Loading—Overall Shop Status

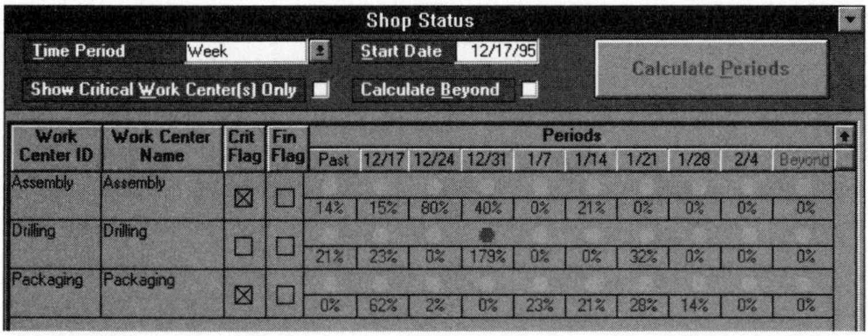

available capacity of a work center during scheduling. If the capacity is already allocated, the system will move the order forward or backward, depending on the scheduling rule, to find an available spot. Since computers are very good at calculating numbers, computing and scheduling according to this rule is computationally easy. However, real life sometimes gets in the way with less-than-precise estimates of the routing times, utilization factors, and efficiency factors. When the three are multiplied together and then used to compute exactly the load for the plant, the schedule can be precisely built on some very shaky ground. Understanding the underlying accuracy of the data and assumptions made during the development of the routings will enhance the utilization of this valuable tool of finite loading. In reality, the best application for finite loading is a machine-constrained situation where the routing times are determined with a high level of precision. Machine-intensive process industries are an excellent application for finite scheduling. This type of industry will schedule the capacity first and then feed this information back to the material plan rather than the other way around. Figure 9–8 is the same work order displayed in Figure 9–7 now loaded in a finite manner. Very different loads are seen in each of the work centers.

The drilling department no longer has a critical problem. The utilization of all departments has leveled considerably. The downside is that the planned lead times for the parts have extended

**FIGURE  9–8**

Finite Loading

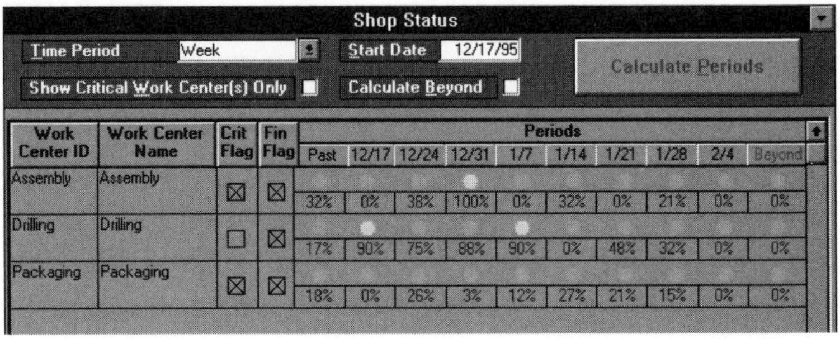

**Shop Status**

| Time Period | Week | | Start Date | 12/17/95 | Calculate Periods |
| Show Critical Work Center(s) Only ■ | | | Calculate Beyond ■ | | |

| Work Center ID | Work Center Name | Crit Flag | Fin Flag | Periods | | | | | | | | | |
| --- | --- | --- | --- | --- | --- | --- | --- | --- | --- | --- | --- | --- | --- |
| | | | | Past | 12/17 | 12/24 | 12/31 | 1/7 | 1/14 | 1/21 | 1/28 | 2/4 | Beyond |
| Assembly | Assembly | ☒ | ☒ | 32% | 0% | 38% | 100% | 0% | 32% | 0% | 21% | 0% | 0% |
| Drilling | Drilling | ☐ | ☒ | 17% | 90% | 75% | 88% | 90% | 0% | 48% | 32% | 0% | 0% |
| Packaging | Packaging | ☒ | ☒ | 18% | 0% | 26% | 3% | 12% | 27% | 21% | 15% | 0% | 0% |

significantly. The reality is the actual lead times haven't changed; they are just better represented in the plan. In Figure 9–7 little demand for capacity existed past January 21. In Figure 9–8 substantial capacity is needed after this date.

This approach to scheduling has been received with expectations of great results and resolutions of problems. Intuitively, finite scheduling should provide a better answer than infinite loading. Now, let's talk about the real world. Only when the setup, run times, and available capacity are extremely accurate and reliable does the process work well. A big problem faced by the typical small manufacturer is the variability in times for setup, run, and available capacity. Learning curve can also play a part as people become more experienced in producing the product. Just knowing who will show up for work the next day can be a big challenge. One person can make a big difference in the output of a small plant. If a single individual does not show up for work or if a slow or fast person is assigned to a particular job, the capacity can be different. Installing a finite loading system does not solve those root core problems. Spending a significant amount of money installing a finite scheduling system is a poor investment for a plant with unreliable routing times and resource availability. These critical resources can be better spent reducing the variability of the production process. This will enhance the overall throughput of the plant far better than the purchase and implementation of a high-priced finite loading program. Once again, the answer is not in automation but in understanding and resolving the root cause of the problem.

## CAPACITY FEEDBACK AND CONTROL

After capacity has been planned, feedback to the plan is required to close the loop. Demonstrated capacity is the proven capacity calculated from actual performance data. This can vary from the planned capacity based on a number of factors such as product mix, process problems, employee training, and other unexpected problems. Adjustments to the efficiency factors are done through examination of the past demonstrated capacity. If the actual output is consistently less than the expected output, the efficiency factor needs to be adjusted downward. Conversely, if the actual output is consistently more than the expected output, the efficiency should be adjusted upward. Remember that efficiency is only a guide to the accuracy of the routing hours estimate, not a performance measure. Attempting to use efficiency as a performance measure causes undesirable behavior where hours are charged to incorrect jobs and other tampering is done to the system to make the measure look good. Combining manufacturing lots to avoid a setup will make the efficiency numbers look good, but the resulting inventory is expensive. The focus on capacity management should be on the capacity process, not on the people involved. Processes, not people, can be controlled.

Capacity control is essential for any production shop. If too many orders are sent to the shop floor, lead time increases as parts sit in queue waiting to be run. Promises to customers are broken as lead times become unpredictable. Orders are released even earlier in hopes of making the desired completion date. Expediting is done to ensure certain orders ship on time, pushing other orders out of the way and into an ever worsening schedule position. Overall planned lead times increase, and even more work orders are released earlier. More work orders are on the shop floor, further muddying the picture and deteriorating lead times. The overall utilization of the formal system begins to break down, and the informal system resumes control.

To cover shortages, substantial dollars are invested in safety stocks of raw materials before they are really needed, adversely impacting cash flow. What a bleak picture! Using a few simple tools, this negative picture can be turned positive.

Input/output control can be used to keep the amount of work in process on the shop floor constant. When the shop floor backlog is constant, lead times are relatively constant and commitments to customers are easier to make. The input/output control process only releases as much work to the shop as is completed during that time period. The focus of input/output control should be on the main bottleneck of the plant. The input/output tool prevents the stratification of work in progress into active, inactive, and sludge.

Active work are the orders where all the components are available and the manufacturing process can be completed. These orders tend to get worked on first and have the shortest lead times through the shop.

Inactive orders are those that need some assistance to be completed either due to a parts shortage or a process problem. These orders are only worked on when the active order base is depleted or someone comes looking for them. They have longer-than-expected lead times.

Sludge are orders that no one wants to touch and everyone wishes would go away. Unfortunately, ignoring them does not make them go away. Due to capacity constraints, these orders are not considered unless they are really needed and are significantly past due. Top levels of management are required to break these orders loose from their resting place. Lead times for these orders can be many times the expected lead times. For these orders to move, the underlying process or material problem must be addressed and resolved. If the answers were easy, the orders would have never deteriorated into this state. The amount of resource required to free these orders may exceed the value of the order. Allowing a high level of work in process on the shop floor encourages these orders to be ignored and the problem to escalate.

Attempting to do input/output control at every work center is not advisable. Once again, the reality of the bottleneck arises. This work area should be closely monitored for output and load. Using a simple Pareto analysis, only 20 percent of the work centers should be closely monitored using input/output control. Practical experience has shown that the number is really closer to 10 percent. A small number of work centers make a big difference in overall schedule performance.

Other tools in capacity control are analyzing future needs for capacity and scheduling orders to smooth future lumpy demands. Customers rarely will order so that the load on the plant is level. Skilled master schedulers can revise the master production schedule so that the customer demands are met and the capacity is more evenly balanced. Even using both methods of loading in Figures 9–7 and 9–8, the result is an extremely lumpy load on the shop. Finite scheduling is not a guarantee of level loads. The master scheduler must integrate all the parts into an effective production schedule.

## SUMMARY

Capacity planning, management, and control are essential to the overall success of the company. Closing the priority planning loop with effective capacity planning yields a powerful reality check. Capacity planning is accomplished by selecting the constraint to increased production. When the bottlenecks to increased production are identified and managed, overall throughput in the plant increases. Every resource does not need to be planned and scheduled, only those impacting the throughput of the operation.

Typically the implementation of a formal planning system will have the capacity planning activity come on line some time after the material planning activity has been stabilized. Too many times, the implementation never gets around to bringing this valuable tool into use. The requirements for effective capacity planning are not complex or difficult. Similar to MRP, the most difficult part is the data input accuracy. The benefits of closed-loop capacity planning far outweigh the investment. Capacity planning validates the overall priority plan and can ensure long-term utilization of the formal planning system by providing essential visibility of future problems. When this begins to happen, the organization moves from reactive fire fighting to proactive, process-focused fire prevention.

# 10

# THE RIGHT TOOLS FOR THE JOB

## ESSENTIAL TOOLS

A screwdriver can be used to insert or remove a screw. A hammer can build or destroy. In the same way, the application of MRP and CRP tools must change to fit the needs of the business. MRP and CRP can be used effectively to manage any manufacturing company. Planning future purchases provides the opportunity for substantial savings in material costs. Providing visibility to suppliers of future requirements allows them to plan their production around known demands rather than abandoning them to the uncertainty of forecasting. The result of this certainty of demand is decreased safety stock and safety capacity. The benefits of this improved planning for the supplier are returned to the customer through lower prices. Using resources to build only what is needed reduces costs for the supplier and therefore price to the customer. CRP provides visibility of the demands and timing for capacity requirements to carry out the master schedule. Options for the best plan of attack can be proactively developed to address these changing capacity needs under less stressful conditions. Integrating the material and capacity plan throughout the supply chain enhances success and profits for every link. No longer must we rely on forecasts with all their inherent inaccuracies; the future can be planned. Since this planning allows the safe removal of safety stocks and other decoupling inventory, the overall supply chain is more responsive to the market and everyone becomes more profitable—a win-win-win situation for the plants, its suppliers, and its customers.

Timely feedback from the shop floor provides meaningful improvement opportunities and essential management information. The biggest benefit of this type of system is proactive planning for the future rather than reacting to the present and the past. Any problem, no matter how large, can be addressed with a possible success plan before it becomes a crisis. Planning and execution tools in the manufacturing arena have changed dramatically over the years with changes in technology and increased worldwide competition.

In the early 1980s, when Just-in-Time manufacturing (JIT) was first making news, most practitioners thought that once JIT was installed, MRP and CRP systems would be obsolete. For the 1990s, the "new" tools include the Theory of Constraints (TOC), Total Quality Management (TQM), Computer-Integrated Manufacturing (CIM), and ISO 9000. Once again, many believe that MRP is old and no longer needed. This could not be more wrong! When sports teams turn out for the first practice of the season, the drill is always the same. They focus on the basics like running, kicking, hitting, and blocking. All the advanced plays are built on the firm foundation of basic controls. Without the strong foundation, the team loses.

MRP and CRP provide the strong foundation for other systems. The most important success factor for MRP implementation is accurate, timely data. Accurate data are also essential for JIT. As lead times get shorter and material replenishment is closely tied to the need, knowing how much is in inventory in real time becomes critical to the whole operation. The bill of materials must be 100 percent accurate to allow this rapid replenishment to occur reliably with the correct parts. Since JIT operations are linked with very little inventory, when material is not available on time, the whole operation stops. Handling product changes or configuration updates can be a challenge due to these short lead times. JIT can use MRP to order long lead materials and provide visibility of these future product change requirements. This future planning visibility is always important, no matter how quickly the plan is executed.

## MRP

MRP is a logical planning system that calculates net requirements from gross requirements for dependent demand items. Requirements are exploded through bills of material from top-level independent demand items and are netted against current on-hand and on-order balances. The requirements are determined for items that must be purchased or made. MRP attempts to drive inventory to zero by providing material to manufacturing precisely when it is needed. In short, MRP provides the planning logic necessary to make or buy only what is needed, when it is needed. This is what many people thought was new about JIT in the 1970s—finally only the inventory that is needed when it is needed. The concept has existed since the 1960s in the original concept of MRP. Implementation of MRP using lot sizes greater than the need, safety stock, and safety lead time were the root cause of the excess inventory in the operation. Inventory is the effect—not the cause. This extra inventory was planned into the process to cover process problems and allow the manufacturing process to continue. When run according to its basic roots, MRP was really the first material JIT system.

Time phasing of deliveries from both internal and external vendors was a big step forward in the field of inventory control. The advent of computers made drastic master schedule changes easier to handle. Now these changes could easily be incorporated into the material and capacity plan. Continued advances in this technology have redefined how we use these basic tools. Daily dispatch lists and priorities can be generated for the shop floor with great detail. MRP is really a simple material and priority planning tool. Some people involved with the first successful implementations thought this simple system could solve all the ills of the company. The limitations of MRP are not in how it calculates the net requirements, but in the accuracy of the inputs fed to the system. The master schedule may not be feasible because there may be insufficient capacity to accomplish the plan. MRP will accurately calculate the requirements to achieve this top-level plan, no matter how grossly overstated. A need in the production and inventory control field was answered by MRP. The computer tool allowed deep-level bills of material and schedule changes to be handled with ease and simplicity. MRP is not an execution tool, but an excellent planning tool. Actions are recommended to a human planner to execute or ignore. The real usefulness of any MRP system is not in the mathematical formulae, but in the skill of the planner and how the system is applied to the business.

## MRP II

MRP II, with its closed financial planning loop, requires MRP. This was the next logical step in the progression of materials planning and control. Consideration is also given to the capacity of the plant in terms of people, machines, cash, square footage, or other resources to ensure the feasibility of the top-level production plan. Accounting is much easier in a manufacturing operation that is in good control. The actions on the production shop floor automatically create accounting transactions that post to the general ledger. No longer must production accounting be completed through arduous manual analysis of work orders and purchase orders each month. Routine daily electronic transactions create automatic journal entries that can be reviewed and analyzed immediately. Any unexpected variances are resolved immediately. By using an iterative trial-and-error planning process, MRP II overcame many shortcomings of an MRP system alone. Figure 10–1 is a graphical representation of this integrated planning and execution system.

The multiple feedback loops between functional areas are the true nuts and bolts of a successful implementation. Now it is possible to plan the work and have everyone working the same plan. Constructive interaction replaces the interfunctional mistrust and second-guessing that occurred previously. This is consistent with the total quality management approach of including all affected parties in the planning of activities. Accurate status within the system is a natural by-product of daily use and dependency on the information. This information is used by everyone, and daily decisions are made using these data. Keeping the data accurate is a key success strategy.

Implementation of a MRP II system is a very complex, involved procedure that requires technical and political exper-

FIGURE   10-1

MRP II

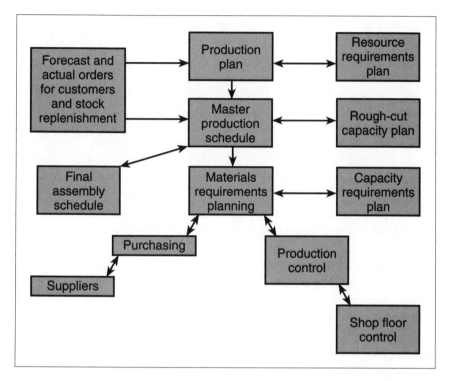

tise. For this reason, even though many companies have MRP installed, MRP II is still a growing phenomenon, and MRP II packages are blossoming in number. Recently, the name has been changed to ERP, enterprise resource planning, to better communicate the extensive breadth of this planning tool. The software companies would have us believe that ERP is something new and different. The functionality of an ERP system is identical to the functionality of a modern MRP II system. The salesperson will attempt to compare the new ERP system with the MRP II systems of old. This is like comparing the functionality of the next Dodge show car to the Edsel—hardly a valid comparison. Both fulfill the same need—getting a human from one point to another in a seated position; however, the Dodge show car does it easier and faster. In the same way, technology has changed, and so have

MRP systems, no matter what the salespeople call it—MRP II or ERP. Also, since so many systems are now installed and helping companies to be more profitable, more is understood about the application of this powerful business tool.

## Just in Time (JIT)

After World War II, Japan began to surpass the United States in terms of productivity gains and quality. "Made in Japan" came to mean quality goods produced at an extremely competitive price, even including inbound shipping and customs fees. The United States began to lose its competitive edge to the country that it helped rebuild. American manufacturing managers began to look for help to rebuild their once-profitable plants. The first reaction was to copy what was obviously successful for the Japanese without fully understanding the underlying philosophy of their tools. Many practitioners believed that JIT could be implemented by purchasing a new piece of software. This misconception was furthered by many software manufacturers that advertised "JIT software." "JIT suppliers" offered to buy and hold inventory and ship to the company "JIT."

This focus on inventory as the cause of the problem was inherently wrong. These implementation efforts were less than successful because JIT is not just another computerized planning system, but a philosophy. Inventory is a result of the problems in the process, not the root problem. Some thought that JIT was just another program of the day that would fade with time. Others felt that JIT was the magic remedy for all the ills of American manufacturing. The real truth is that JIT manufacturing was the real beginning of the total quality management movement and reengineering focus that would develop in the 1990s.

The JIT philosophy can be viewed as a relentless, never-ending crusade of respect for people and the total elimination of waste. This must occur not only in the manufacturing process, but throughout the total organization for the implementation to be successful. The direct results are easier to see in the production facility, but the results in the other support areas are as important. By-products of a JIT implementation are a major reduction in lead time, inventory, and required space, yielding a more competitive company. The savings are not the direct cost of the inventory or space. The true savings are in alternate uses of these critical resources to increase the overall success of the company. This goal is not achieved by installation of a new computer program; it is achieved by the cooperative effort of everyone in the company, from the president to the line workers. Human resources are fully utilized throughout the organization. New systems have to be developed to accommodate the new manner of business. Work orders, shop paper, and generally accepted cost accounting practices have been modified. Activity-based costing recognizes the fallacies of traditional cost accounting and attempts to provide a more meaningful financial analysis of the business. These tactics and measurements are still undergoing dramatic changes as a result of this major philosophical concept.

## TOOLS OF THE 1990s

Newer tools like the theory of constraints, Computer-Integrated Manufacturing, TQM, and ISO 9000 also fit into this integrated toolbox. These tools were developed to answer specific needs and issues that began arising in the company. Worldwide competition, shortened supply chains, and customer pressure to decrease prices and lead times were the catalysts for developing these new tools. No longer can we do what we have always done and be content with what we have always gotten. The environment has changed and the rules of the game have changed with it. New tools are needed to become and stay competitive in these new markets.

### Theory of Constraints

During the time that companies were attempting to copy the Japanese, an Israeli physicist, Eli Goldratt, was taking a hard look at the goals and procedures in the organization. His recommendations for action were introduced in an easily understood book, *The Goal*. This book introduced a new philosophy termed theory of constraints (TOC). Anyone working in manufacturing that reads this book swears that the book was written about the company. Common sense tells us that the main goal of any company is to make money. Achieving that goal is more than common sense and luck. Many roadblocks prevent the company from accomplishing that result. Bottlenecks restrict the ability of the company to increase profits. Bottlenecks are constraints to the process. Capacity at the bottleneck is, by definition, less than the load. If the bottleneck is allowed to run out of work, the entire system produces less output. Bottlenecks are fairly easy to spot in a production job shop. Take a walk out to the shop floor and look where the biggest pile of inventory is sitting. This is the machine that is holding up the work and always seems to be operating to Murphy's law. This is the bottleneck of the operation.

The bottleneck may not even be on the shop floor. Take a similar walk through the paperwork process. Look for the backup of work at one station. Again, this is the bottleneck. The output of the whole system is dependent on the productivity of this bottleneck. Preceding work centers are capable of feeding this bottleneck in excess of what the bottleneck can produce. Subsequent work centers can flush through the work as it is produced through the bottleneck. Standard Capacity Requirements Planning (CRP) computer systems for scheduling work center capacity can still be used. Routings and schedules are simplified to focus on the bottleneck. Operations prior to the bottleneck are pulled by the activity at the bottleneck. MRP logic determines the sequence and configuration of the production at the bottleneck. Work in process after the bottleneck is handled by flexible capacity. The largest change occurs by focusing on the bottleneck of the process and realizing that cost savings in increased efficiency at nonbottleneck resources are just a mirage.

This focus utilizes the concepts and tools of total quality management to optimize the production through this bottleneck. The work is critically examined. Any nonvalue-added steps are removed. Simplification of the remaining work will also increase the throughput. When the bottleneck has been fully optimized, the bottleneck may even be broken and may no longer be the bottleneck. One great truth is that when one bottleneck is broken, another forms to take its place. The best priority for company process improvement is achieved through sequential examination and improvement of bottleneck operations. Similar to JIT and MRP II, all areas must be involved during the planning, implementation, and execution for maximum success. Standard accounting techniques can be used to evaluate cost savings because the attention is on the bottleneck that, by definition, must run at full capacity. The theory of constraints recognizes that the overhead or cost driver is this bottleneck resource. Activity-based costing can be used to evaluate the overall effectiveness and cost impact of the improvement efforts. The theory of constraints is not so much a change in technology or systems, but a shift in focus. Once this shift in focus has been made, the focus on bottlenecks seems like common sense. This shift is all too uncommon.

## Computer-Integrated Manufacturing (CIM)

CIM is the technological ultimate in the computerization of manufacturing planning, control, and execution systems. In the 1970s, the vision of the futuristic plant was total automation and robotics. Reality set in and the importance of human resource was realized. Even so, Computer-Integrated Manufacturing can provide a competitive advantage when properly executed. Extensive planning is required for this large investment to have a positive cash flow within the desired return period. Similar to JIT, a problem surrounds the basic understanding of Computer-Integrated Manufacturing (CIM). CIM is not a turnkey product that can be purchased off the shelf. The automation process must be tailored to each company. CIM is an all-encompassing view of a business fully utilizing and integrating its computer resources. Planning a CIM installation requires a meticulous examination of the firm and its markets. An analysis is completed on how the firm will serve those markets now and in the future.

The advent of CIM reinforces the need for long-term planning. At the installation of the first islands of computerization, a blueprint is required to ensure communication is possible with later additions. Having independent islands of automation unable to communicate causes higher expense and extreme frustration. CIM can lower costs for prototypes and production pieces by significantly reducing or eliminating setup times and limiting the proliferation of part numbers. Parts designed on a computer-aided design system can be run immediately on a compatible computer-aided manufacturing system. The need for prototypes to check for fit and function is replaced with a 3-D computer fit-up. The time and cost savings can be significant. The most important and outstanding benefit for a company that has successfully implemented CIM is the flexibility to quickly accommodate the changing needs of the marketplace. This rapid response capability can be used as a competitive strategic tool.

## Total Quality Management (TQM)

Total quality management (TQM) was introduced during the 1980s and early 1990s as the latest answer to the problem of worldwide competitiveness. TQM focused on process control and continuous improvement. Once again, an essential tool is back under a new name. JIT also focuses on the process and the elimination of any unnecessary resources consumed by a process. Many different quality experts developed and taught their own definition of quality. One thread was continuous throughout—a focus on the customer and their expectations, needs, and wants. No longer can we depend on inspection to validate quality. Inspection proved to be expensive and ineffective. Process control became the key word. Having processes capable of producing only parts that meet expectations reduces overall operating cost and improves profits.

The ideas of TQM further evolved into the reengineering movement. Reengineering examines all the business processes and questions why tasks are being done and what value they add. The key to all process improvements is the process owners—people—the same resource that makes any planning system a success. This quality movement brought into clear focus that the problem is not the people but the process. The people have the answers for the process problems. TQM helped ask the right questions to get these answers.

## ISO 9000

Another trend of the 1990s is the movement towards ISO 9000. Again, this is a logical evolution of existing tools. TQM focused on the process. ISO 9000 is a set of guidelines for documenting the process and assuring that this process is followed. Many customers, especially in Europe, began to understand how expensive multiple audits of suppliers had become. Suppliers were answering the same questions for many different customers. Independent ISO 9000 audit firms provide the same result with only one audit. The goal of the audit is the same. Is the process understood by all operators and is the process documented? Was the process followed? How do you know the process was followed? ISO 9000 is not a guarantee of quality, just consistency. Similar to the other business tool developments, the first to embrace this concept were rewarded with a market advantage. As more companies achieve the ISO 9000 certification, it has become a requirement to do business.

## COMBINING THE TOOLS

Installing and maintaining an accurate MRP system teaches valuable lessons to all involved with the system. Data accuracy and overall control of material flow are imperative when attempting to progress to more advanced concepts. The practices of cycle counting and overall quality controls are part of any good inventory control process. A successful implementation of MRP is an excellent building block for the future. MRP II builds on many skills that were learned during the MRP phase and adds emphasis to interfunctional communication. A successful implementation of MRP II may require a shift in company organization and communication channels. This increased communication and visibility make MRP II a great advance in the field. The practice of planning the work and having everyone work the same plan is a big step forward.

When JIT is implemented, a major shift in focus occurs in the execution function. The bill of material is flattened and simplified. Parts are grouped by similar production processes. Capacity is dedicated to the production of these product groups. Dissimilar machines are brought into small areas called manufacturing cells. Manufacturing cells now handle in one routing step what previously was accomplished with a multitude of routings, material moves, and queues. Short lead times through the cell result in dramatic reductions in work in process inventory. This inventory reduction in turn allows rapid identification of problems. Whenever inventory declines suddenly between operations, downstream operations are starved, making visibility of the problem immediate. Resources can then be mobilized immediately to solve the problem. The master scheduler no longer needs to decouple manufacturing and the market with finished goods inventory because JIT allows successful synchronous building matched to the demands of the market. The master schedule now serves the long-term function of providing future visibility of production rates. Due to shorter lead times, marketing is no longer held under the gun to predict market consumption with perfect accuracy well into the future (an impossible feat anyway!). The planning horizon is shortened due to the reduction of lead times throughout the entire supply chain.

The Theory of Constraints (TOC) builds on many requirements of JIT and MRP but concentrates on the identification of bottlenecks. This theory concentrates on spending critical capacity to build only what is required for the market when it is required. Flexibility to answer customer demand is one benefit. No matter what the business environment, the theory of constraint logic can be applied.

## TOOL APPLICATION

These different tool combinations must fit the needs of the business. Each business is unique. Attempting to copy tool application exactly from a successful competitor usually results in failure. Each company culture, leadership style, and market segment combination require that the tools be selected and integrated differently. Successful businesses select from the toolbox only the tools that are needed and use them in a way that benefits the business. Some common characteristics are present based on the type of business to begin the choice of tools.

### Remanufacturing

This is probably one of the most difficult environments to run on an MRP system. Traditional MRP plans all the components required to put something together. The remanufacturer's first step is to take something apart. The requirements for each order can be dramatically different. This type of business still uses MRP to plan material replenishment by using "best guess" bills of material and routings for a "typical" part. Remembering that this practice is really forecasting and since forecasts are always wrong, this practice is inherently variable in its output. To guard against this variability, investments are made in safety stock for parts and safety capacity for resources. Inventory control is a challenge since the process is not consistent and unidirectional. The remanufacturing process doubles back on itself many times during normal processing. Things are taken apart and must be carefully tracked through their individual processes to be reinstalled when the unit is rebuilt. Place this confusing inventory process in a functional job shop and the management nightmare begins.

One way to simplify the process is to tightly control the amount of work in process to ensure a stable lead time. Grouping similar product groups into production cells simplifies the overall process since parts tracking becomes easier. The master scheduler plans projected capacity and material usage based on a projection of typical parts. The basic control tools required in MRP are essential in this environment, since a single part can stop a whole unit from shipping.

## Continuous Process

Unlike the batch manufacturer, continuous process is a never-ending run, usually on a single machine. This type of manufacturing is used for paper mills and oil refineries. Typically this type of manufacturing is equipment intensive, and the capacity is determined by machine-hours. Continuous process uses CIM extensively to feed back critical performance measures on the process and make real-time corrections. Due to the level of capital investment involved, the continuous process manufacturer tends to be a large company. The products produced are extremely high in volume and have little or no variety. The continuous process manufacturer competes in the market on price, and the product is really a commodity. MRP is still useful to plan the needed raw materials, but this planning is quite simple and can often be done on a simple spreadsheet. The complexity of this type of process is ensuring the reliability of the equipment. One hiccup causes the whole line to shut down. The machines are usually very expensive to start up and shut down so shutdowns are planned well into the future. The long setup times are not an issue to the plant response time to the customer since the product variety is negligible. The production rates are very high, and the cycle times are very low. Schedules for the customer can be done with a high degree of certainty depending on the reliability of the machine. This industry type is the best application for finite scheduling and rate-based MRP.

## Batch

A batch operation has the characteristics of a repetitive shop with some of the end-item varieties of the job shop. The manufacturing process is repetitive, but the output can be very different. The batch has a definitive beginning and end. The batch process produces a discrete amount of output that can be counted. In a batch plant, the bills of material are optimized for a certain batch size. This can be due to the requirements of the machines used in the production process or to the nature of the product itself. As a consequence, the materials are planned in these fixed-lot batch sizes. If a larger batch is required than normal, two batches will be made. Just like in baking, doubling a recipe in a single mix does not always work. Scaling a batch operation can require extensive research and testing to ensure the output will meet expectations. Batch operations usually entail the strictest of traceability requirements due to the products normally made in this approach. Examples of batch operations are food manufacturers, pharmaceutical manufacturers, and medical device manufacturers. Many times these manufacturers believe that they are process industries, but the output is really in batches. This type of manufacturing has the process simplicity of the repetitive manufacturer but the paperwork requirements of the job shop. Traceability of material batches to an end-item batch number is required. Bills of material are relatively flat. Common components can make a multitude of different end items. Routings usually contain only a few steps. The main concern of this type of manufacturing is to ensure timely availability of resources needed for the continuous processing and lot tracking. Work in process and finished goods are kept relatively low due to the shelf life of the products. Process reliability is essential for the success of the batch manufacturer. The overall approach to batch manufacturing is to use MRP to plan materials and configurations and JIT execution tools to simplify the control process, where possible. CRP gives an overall plan for critical resource demands.

## Repetitive Shop

A repetitive manufacturer makes high-volume products in low variety. Medical device manufacturers, electronic assemblers, and other high-volume production facilities accomplish the conversion process through a series of fixed sequential operations. Work in process is low, and these operations are highly dependent on each other. Fitting repetitive manufacturing into job shop computer systems is possible. The difficulty is reducing the amount of paperwork and transactions. If the same amount of paperwork and transaction is used to build repetitive product as discrete product in a job shop, the production workforce is soon buried under mountains of paper. Since product is built in high volume, the goal is to reduce the detail level of progress reporting since this feedback does not add value, only cost. The reduced level of work in process simplifies the control and reporting systems. Some software companies have developed true repetitive systems. Traditional systems can still be used with some minor modifications. One method is to plan production in weekly rate-based buckets. The traditional system then does all the background planning and transactions that would have been completed for a job shop. The processing time and computing power required is much larger than expected for the number of transactions entered. True repetitive systems have simplified the internal processing of the system to really reflect the overall manufacturing process.

The repetitive product is characterized by high volumes and very low variety. The raw materials needed are repetitious in quantity and timing. The end items are still discrete but are produced in a very short cycle time. The management of this type of operation turns to balancing the capacity along the line rather than planning detailed routings. The bills of material tend to be very flat. Routings are simple, with only one or two steps. Costs for this type of operation are easy to allocate directly to the line. The "four wall approach" is used to track inventory. Receipts are transacted when the product arrives, and deductions are made to the inventory when the final product leaves. Intermediate tracking does not add value to the process, only cost, so this tracking is not done. JIT execution tools such as *kanban* are used to bring materials to the line. Empty containers are sent to the supplier to be filled when they are empty. The supplier then refills the container and sends it back to the line.

Sometimes the product is not repetitive but the process is. The same repetitive tools can be used for a final assembly operation where many different configurations of parts are running down the same line. MRP can be linked into the execution side to determine the configuration and line sequence order of the replenishment container. The empty container still authorizes a replenishment, and MRP schedules the configuration of the parts. The repetitive operation is the most simple to comprehend, yet it can be the most difficult to manage. Any unexpected breakdown can cause the entire plant to shut down. The positive side is that there are not piles of inventory covering up the problems. A sense of urgency is common in the identification and resolution of the problems encountered in this type of facility.

## Project (Complex) Manufacturing

When the company works on large, one-time projects, the production environment is considered project or complex manufacturing. These projects tend to be similar in type to previous projects handled by the company, but each new project is unique in its requirements. This type of manufacturing process is found in construction and engineer-to-order companies. The lead time in this environment is even longer than the job shop. Not only are material and capacity planned, but activities are planned for projected need and completion. A key process feedback requirement in this business environment is a projected cost to complete the project. Project management tools are used to provide the planning and feedback visibility. Project management tools follow the same logic as MRP but allow slack time between operations that still support the desired completion date. Early start and early finish dates can be calculated. These are the earliest dates that an activity can take place. Late start and late finish dates are the last dates by which the activity must be done to support the schedule. When the early and late dates are the same, the activity is on the critical path. MRP by definition places everything on the critical path with no slack.

The major concern in the project management environment is to have quality material on hand when it is needed. Flexibility in start dates between the early start and late start dates complicates this planning. Not having the material when needed can delay the entire project and cost substantial money. The material is usually unique to the project, and therefore a safety stock of inventory is not found in the company. The planning for the company also includes a projection of the critical resources needed to increase the level of business. If this critical resource is highly specialized scientists or researchers, the time to procure this resource can be quite long.

The bills of material and routings are developed as the product is defined. The difficulty is that the product is usually developed and defined from top down. The production process occurs and requirements begin from the bottom up. This dichotomy of requirements increases the lead time needed to create this unique finished product. MRP plans from top down, but the bills of material under the make items must be defined down to the purchased items for the plan to be really useable. Routings are established in the same way as a job shop, after the design and specifications have been completed for the parts. CIM can be very beneficial in this type of environment. The tight integration of design and manufacturing drastically reduces the lead time for manufacturing.

## Job Shop

The typical small business is a job shop. A job shop is characterized by different groups of similar machines producing a high variety of output. Movement between the machines can be in any sequence needed to complete the desired output. The product mix is relatively low in volume but high in variety. The key

strategic factor for a job shop is maximum flexibility and availability of capacity. Lead times to the customer are relatively long.
As a result, the work in process is comparatively high. Job shops
usually produce in response to a direct customer order. The customer provides a blueprint and specification for the job. The job
shop usually produces parts for the OEM (original equipment
manufacturer) assembly operation. The small business job shop
rarely produces product that is sold directly to the end user.

This environment was the application for which Material
Requirements Planning was originally developed. The flexible
routings require more control and focus on detailed capacity planning than any other type of production. The master scheduler
focuses on balancing the demand for and availability of capacity
while servicing the customer's need. The Theory of Constraints
fits this type of production very well. If the product mix stays stable, the bottlenecks in the operation tend to be in the same work
area. As the underlying product mix changes, the bottleneck can
move from one area to another. This possibility is easily identified proactively through Capacity Requirements Planning.

In an effort to keep the lead time to the customer shorter than
the total cumulative lead time, forecasts are done for capacity and
critical component material requirements. These component materials may be stocked to allow quicker response to an incoming customer order. Remembering the number one rule of forecasts is that
forecasts are always wrong, shorter lead times in this flexible plant
can dramatically enhance the overall success of the company. These
shorter lead times may be possible by building only what the customer orders when the parts are ordered, rather than grouping
batches of parts together. The main driver for manufacturing lot
sizes greater than the current need is setup time. When a large setup time exists for a part, the rational thought is to produce a larger
batch to conserve costs. These larger batches increase the level of
work in process and in turn the lead time. Smaller batches decrease
the level of work in process and lead time. In turn, this simplifies
the overall management process. Gathering similar setups together
to reduce setup time and therefore overall lead time is one way to
economically reduce batch size. Grouping parts that follow similar manufacturing processes into production cells also reduces the
work in process and overall lead time. As the lead times are reduced,

the tools and systems required are significantly less complex. JIT tools can be used to sequence the production in the job shop with a rather fixed flow. As work is completed through a work center, the authorization is done to release more work to that center equal to the hours completed. This stabilization of work in process levels results in stabilized lead times through the plant. Similar to how a *kanban* releases more material to a repetitive line, load can be released to the plant through a pull system.

The biggest benefit of MRP implementation in the job shop is the forward visibility of material and capacity demands. Since the main concern for small business is cash flow, this visibility translates directly into projected cash flow analysis. Shortening the time required for manufacturing has a positive direct impact on the cash flow. Focusing on improving overall product flow has direct beneficial financial results.

## SUMMARY

On one hand, all these business environments are very different. On the other hand, these businesses are very much the same. Every business takes inputs, adds values, and then creates outputs. Management of the resources and materials needed to add that value is the task of the different tools in the management toolbox—MRP, CRP, TOC, TQM, CIM, JIT—and a whole horde of other TLAs (three-letter acronyms). These tool names may look like vegetable soup, but, when well understood and effectively utilized, they can create a strategic advantage for the company. Understanding the requirements and philosophies of each of these tools is relatively easy. The real difficulty is understanding the application and integration of these tools. Different philosophical purists deny the usability of some of the other tools and declare their particular specialty as the only true answer. The real artistry comes in taking the best from each and combining them in synergy to answer the needs of the company, regardless of size. Many small businesses are successfully competing with large businesses using these unique integrated applications. Experience has shown that when these tools are well understood and used to create a unique system that truly fits the needs of the business and its customers, that business can become a world-class competitor, no matter what its size.

# 11

## SYSTEM SELECTION AND IMPLEMENTATION

### INTRODUCTION

Selecting the MRP software and integrating it into the business can be an overwhelming experience. Commercially available material requirements planning systems are plentiful. These systems run on a variety of hardware and operating systems. In reality, 80 to 90 percent of all the system features and functions are the same. The 10 to 20 percent that make them different are unique characteristics due to operating system, hardware, or features. If a certain system has the unique features needed for your business, that system will be easier to implement. Specialty systems have been developed to meet the needs of different market segments like remanufacturing, repetitive, and complex manufacturing. If the system does not have these unique features, implementation is still possible but just more difficult. Many companies blame poor results on the software. Rarely is the software at fault. All currently available commercial software completes the gross-to-net MRP calculation correctly. The difference between success and failure is the implementation process.

With the purchase of a material requirements planning system, the expectation is a positive financial return on that investment. This return should occur in the near or immediate future, not in five years. Many companies have spent millions of dollars on MRP software, and the results have been disappointing at best. After one system implementation failure, the company picks up the pieces and attempts the process again. Small companies cannot afford even one of these costly errors. The nature of a small business is that one misstep in judgment can cost the whole business. Each organization has a different combination of process and culture. The successful system must be uniquely tailored to that combination. However, one common theme is present for all successful implementations—education, education, education!

## EDUCATION

Education provides the overall understanding of what the company is attempting to implement and why. Many implementations fail because of confusion about how the system will fit into the normal business or how the normal business must change to accommodate system implementation. This confusion manifests itself in data inaccuracy, as the system is not maintained and used. Using the old informal system is easier than learning the new tool that is available, even though the new system makes the job easier. Over time, data inaccuracy grows and grows. Soon the new system has lost all credibility and things are no better than before, as everyone returns to the old system. If this happens, most likely the old system was never really abandoned.

A real possibility exists that things could be even worse—the management team has lost its credibility with the workforce or, even worse, the company cannot continue to operate. How can these dismal possibilities be avoided? The first step on the road to competitiveness is a common understanding of the destination. Every journey is easier when the final destination is well understood and communicated. This common understanding is possible only through education. Rarely does a small company have the resources for an internal trainer. This means that this crucial education must be secured from outside the organization. One excellent supplier of education for this type of implementation comes through an organization called APICS, The Educational Society for Resource Management (for information call 1-800-444-APIC). Using local chapters for cost-effective education, national workshops, and symposia, this organization has standardized the language of manufacturing worldwide. Since 1957, almost all manufacturing control system software has been programmed consistent with the APICS body of knowledge. Although many consultants provide education directly at the plant site, the experiences in the classroom are only from within the company. An APICS educational opportunity provides an opportunity for people from the company to network with other manufacturing people facing the same issues and problems at different companies. These educational opportunities are available at a fraction of the cost of an on-site consultant. Networking for benefiting the common good was the original motivation behind the founding of APICS in 1957. Why reinvent the wheel when someone else is willing to tell you how to build it?

The need for education cannot be stressed too strongly. Imagine entrusting an accountant with no education with the responsibility of preparing financial statements. No sane business owner would make that move. Daily, the same business owners entrust the management of their inventory, the largest portion of current assets, to incompletely trained people. When you consider that the inventory is an asset like cash, educating the workforce to effectively manage this asset does not seem like a luxury. A sage advisor once said: "If you think education is expensive, try ignorance." Education is required for all employees to help in a successful implementation. Well-meaning people can do exactly the wrong thing for the right reasons. Recommended education includes the basics of manufacturing control and a detailed understanding of how MRP systems work. The education program should answer the question, Why?

## TRAINING

In addition to the education required, training is needed to operate the software. This training is typically included directly or indirectly in the purchase price of the software. Training answers the question, How? Software training will teach the people using the system the keystrokes and transactions required to run the company. This training class is an excellent opportunity to network with other users of the software and use their experiences to benefit your company. Typically the instructor of the class is not only an expert in the software, but also has implemented this software in many companies. Feel free to pick his brain for application suggestions and pitfalls associated with the implementation. Given the reduced cost of laptop computers, taking one to this session allows for the immediate application of the class training to your specific company requirements. Your questions can be answered during the class. Attempting to implement software without this type of training is like putting someone behind the controls of an airplane for the first time and encouraging them to fly. The trip can be exciting, but the results can be deadly. Part of the expected support from the software company is the ability to communicate a complete knowledge of the software functionality and limitations in addition to an understanding of how it should be applied to your company.

## PROJECT PLAN

### Determine Needs

The software must answer the needs of the company. But how are these needs identified? All direct users of the system or the system's output should be involved in the development of the needs identification. Needs can be identified in a number of ways.

**Brainstorming Session**
In the brainstorming session all the wants and needs are identified through a technique called normative group. Each person is asked to bring a list of the key requirements for the system. Each person in turn adds one of her ideas to the master list until all the lists have been exhausted. Usually during this process, the addition of items not originally thought of will be made, as each functional area listens to the concerns of other areas. After all the ideas have been consolidated, the list is prioritized into features that must be in the software for the business to run, items that would be great to have, and items that are nice to have. This list forms the basis of the request for proposal that is sent to prospective software suppliers. During the demonstration of the software by the supplier, the issues critical to the business should be demonstrated and well understood.

### Solution Providers

Some of the integrated computer companies provide a service of developing the requirements document for the business so that appropriate fit solutions can be recommended. The cost of this work is usually very reasonable. The downside is that the solutions recommended will most likely be ones that the solution provider carries. If the highest concern for the system selection is to ensure objectivity, do not use the same company to specify a system and to install it. An independent source can be used to determine specifications and recommend possible solutions. Use a different resource to aid in the implementation to ensure independence and objectivity.

### Consulting Services

Many consultants develop and write system specifications. Similar to using solutions providers, beware of using the same consultant to specify and support the implementation of the system. The recommendation made will most probably be one of the systems she represents. Independent quantitative selection services are available that endorse no single system. These services utilize extensive questioning of the current and desired processes and procedures. The answers are then run against a database of responses from the software suppliers. The result is a short list of most likely solutions for the business. An example of this type of independent consulting services is Expert Buying Systems (1-800-832-6434). They endorse no single solution and keep on file hundreds of software companies' responses on system features and functions. When sending a specification document from this type of service, the software company is likely to respond since the software has already been shown to be a possible fit.

## Select Software

Once the specifications have been written, the hard part starts. These wants and needs are documented and sent to prospective software suppliers. A request for proposal is made. Normally the response rate from the prospective software supplier is directly dependent on the research done during the specification development. If requests for proposals are sent only to software companies that are known to fit the overall needs, the response rate will be quite high. However, if the request for proposal is sent out in a shotgun fashion to any known MRP solution provider, the response rate can be less than half. Given the level of effort required to develop the specification document, putting some time and effort into researching potential suppliers is time well spent. Using consulting services or solution providers can facilitate this process.

The number of proposals reviewed should be no more than five. After the responses are received, each response is critically reviewed. At this point, the proposals can be narrowed down to the top three. After the top three are selected, each of these companies is asked to provide a demonstration of its system. Beware of the canned presentation with a script. The sales personnel will attempt to sell you on the sizzle and graphics of the system rather than its real functionality. Clearly communicate to the prospective supplier the unique needs of your business, and ask for a demonstration of those items identified in the proposal as "must have." Remember that commercial software is not likely to fit every need and want for your business perfectly. The task at hand is to select the best fit. Other considerations when selecting software include how long the company has been in business, how many copies of the software have been sold, and how many were successfully installed. A local user's group is a wonderful resource as you begin your implementation. This provides you an opportunity to network with a number of users at different levels of implementation.

Be careful about being a "beta site" for software. Beta sites test the software for bugs and usually receive the software at a significant discount. Given this is a mission critical system, this might be similar to taking advantage of a sale on brain surgery. Understand that there will be trade-offs between the latest and greatest utilization of technology and the number of installed sites. Companies that have been around for a long time tend to have outdated technology and proprietary database structures in their system. The advantage they have is a large, installed customer base, and the code is well tested and very robust. New companies on the scene can have the latest bells and whistles, but without many people running it, the reliability can be severely lacking.

The worst thing that can happen is to purchase your software, begin to implement the system, and have the software provider go out of business. Having this contingency covered in the original contract is a good idea. Many software companies sell to small business through value-added resellers. These independent organizations support the product and receive a payment from the company or directly from the customer for this support. The advantage of this approach is that the support for the software is local. The customer does not have to be concerned with time zone differences between its location and the software supplier. The disadvantage is that the value-added reseller may not know the software as well as the programming company or may run into unrelated business difficulties. Again, this is an excellent contingency to cover in the contract. A quality solution provider will back up its value-added reseller chain in the event it goes out of business. After all this education and all the hard questions have been asked and answered, a software package has been selected. How does it get implemented?

## Implement the System

The first step in implementation is bringing together all the people who will be affected by the system. In a small company, the implementation team is usually the entire user base. Normal time for the implementation should be in the range of three months to one year. The time the implementation will take is directly related to the current condition of the business. If the company is already using unique item identifiers and bills of material and possesses good data accuracy, the implementation can take less than three months. If item identifiers, bills of material, and routings still need to be developed, the time will be closer to one year. Implementations taking more than one year tend to never achieve success. Interest and energy wane with the lack of accomplishment, and the implementation dies.

In the management of an implementation, there are three control knobs: scope, resources, and time. If the scope of the project is reduced, the project will take less time. If the resources are reduced, the time required will be longer. Finding the resources to support the implementation can be the most difficult issue to face. Two successful approaches can be taken. One is to bring in temporary help for routine duties. These temporaries can be low-wage people who perform the repetitive tasks. But supervising temporaries might take more time than they save. Another temporary option is a college intern. These interns are usually well educated but do not have practical experience. They can be used to augment the team during the implementation and are usually very quick in coming up to speed in the organization. This opportunity provides them work experience and the company the extra resources needed at a reasonable price—a winning combination for both parties involved.

The second way to free resources is to begin doing the existing job differently. Each task currently being done must be examined to see if it really adds value to the organization or just adds work. Many people are very busy working hard but accomplish little. Many daily tasks are done without challenging their need because we have always done things that way. The most important part of the implementation process is the reengineering of current processes.

## PROJECT PLAN—MAJOR MILESTONES

### Select Project Team

The project team in a small company is mostly likely the entire user base. If the entire user base is too large for an effective team, select a representative from each functional area with sufficient authority to make decisions. The team should have a common vision of the implementation's goal. These people are responsible for the application of the selected software to their own business environment. The project team should have an extensive understanding of the concept of MRP and a detailed understanding of the software tool. They become the in-house experts who should answer questions as other people begin to use the system. The people selected for this team are not those people who can afford to be away from their regular job to support the implementation. The project team consists of people who are the core of the business. Relieving some of their regular workload is needed to provide the time required for implementation. Skimping on the competency of the project team reflects directly in the implementation results.

## Install and Test Hardware

Before even attempting to use any software, be sure that the hardware is reliable and running as expected. This includes the operating system and any communications links. A common error is to load everything, operating system and applications, onto the new computer at the same time. When the combination does not work, it is almost impossible to determine the cause. The hardware and operating system should be installed well in advance of the beginning of the implementation. Buying bargain-basement hardware is rarely a real bargain. One company recently spent hundreds of hours and thousands of dollars entering and reentering data only to find that a defective (cheap) network card worth less than $100 was corrupting the data faster than it could enter it. Remember, the system being implemented is mission critical for the business. This is probably one of the largest investments made by the company. Skimping on the quality of the hardware usually means many hours of problems and frustration.

## Attend System Training

Each software package has different ways of accomplishing the required tasks. Attending system training is essential in understanding the system and will shorten the overall implementation. Usually the software company provides this training at a reasonable price. Many valuable hints about using the software come out of these classes. Use this class to the maximum potential. A wealth of information is possible from the instructor and fellow participants. Ask how others handled problems currently facing your business. If they successfully overcame those problems, they will be happy to tell how they did it. Also, usually the participants will freely share how they attempted to solve the problem and failed.

## Complete Conference Room Pilot

A conference room pilot exercises the whole system and tests the users' understanding of the system. This step is unwisely skipped in many cases in the hurry to implement the system. The new system goes on line and suddenly no one knows how to ship a part, relieve inventory, and invoice the customer. The conference room pilot provides the opportunity to do all the activities of the business in one focused area.

A good checklist for the conference room pilot is listed below. The people expected to use the system should be able to do the following:

1. Enter a part.
2. Completely define the bills of material.
3. Enter a customer order.
4. Plan needed purchased and make parts.
5. Place a purchase order for a purchase part.
6. Receive a purchased part and enter the invoice.
7. Pay the invoice.
8. Open a manufacturing order.
9. Issue material to the manufacturing order.
10. Report progress on the manufacturing order.
11. Look at the status of the manufacturing order.
12. Complete the manufacturing order and receive to inventory.
13. Ship the product to the customer and send an invoice.
14. Receive cash for the invoice.

These tasks should be completed without hunting and pecking around the system in confusion. Each person must know very clearly how to do the job using the new system. Only when the system is well understood should the implementation move to the next step. Once the standard business processes that are defined in these 14 steps are developed, begin handling the exceptions that happen on a daily basis. The conference room is a better place to work out these issues than the shop floor. The conference room pilot will save many hours and frustration later. This is the beginning of developing the policies and procedures for using the system. Document these policies and procedures as they are developed. This will save time later and will ensure they are completed.

## Set-Up Security and Permissions

Every system has a system of allowing only authorized people to look at and transact portions of the data. These permissions must be developed early on to prevent surprises later in the process. The recommended way to develop security and permissions is to have open permissions during the training phase. This allows everyone to see all the features and functions of the system. During the conference room pilot, begin setting the security and permission definitions to ensure that everyone has what she needs. The risk of waiting until the system is brought on line is that there is a high probability that security settings will not be correct. People may be getting in and "playing with" things they should not be handling, adversely affecting financial reporting. The other possibility is that sufficient permission has not been given to allow the person to do her job and frustration results. Security and permissions are an important part of the conference pilot process.

## Conduct Company-Specific Pilot

If the conference room pilot was done using the supplied test database from the software company, now is the time to enter a few real parts built by the company. These parts should be put through the same 14 steps of the conference pilot. Once the system is well understood, then all the issues and problems that normally arise in daily production can be simulated. Some examples of these problems are inventory adjustments, customer changes, engineering changes, credit holds, machines down, people not showing up, and parts shortages. Be creative in testing scenarios that face the company. Having the entire project team address these issues brings excellent insight to the overall process. Reengineering the process is best during this time.

## Identify Beginning Pilot

If possible, it is preferable not to bring the entire company on-line in one shot. This approach does not allow for incremental correction of errors in processes and procedures. No matter how thorough the planning, the actual implementation will always reveal unexpected problems and issues. Better to have these show up in a slice of the business rather than bringing the entire company to its knees. In addition, the resources required to implement the whole company at once are probably not available. A good way to begin the actual use of the system is to identify a part of the business that can be segregated and brought on line. This allows for the new policies and procedures to be tested in actual use with a minimum data set that people are familiar with before the entire company is committed.

Many small companies attempt to bring up the new system and run the old system in parallel. This approach results in complete overload on the people and often concludes in a failed implementation. The resources to keep the current system running are already consuming all the company's resources. When a second system is added, neither gets the attention nor resources needed. As a result, they both flounder and everyone becomes frustrated. Running a reasonable pilot data set in parallel, while increasing the workload somewhat, allows all users to be fully trained and gain confidence in the system, greatly easing the full company conversion.

Cutting over cold turkey is a gutsy approach best done when several conference room pilots have been completed successfully. This is done in very small companies where the project team is the entire user community. This cold turkey cutover approach also fits a company with a single product line or simple product. The least risk approach is to transfer chunks of the business onto the new system incrementally.

### Enter Static Data

Many systems will allow the automatic transfer of any existing item masters, bills of material, customer masters, vendor masters, and employee masters. If this process can be completed quickly and accurately, it can be a real time saver. However, this process can cause many strange problems later in the implementation. Sometimes the old data are so bad the decision is made to enter the data manually and ensure the accuracy for each segment of the business brought on line. If the amount of data is not overwhelming, keying the data into the new system is usually the best alternative. The system will perform the edits necessary to ensure integrity of the database. These edits are not performed when directly populating the database with uploads of old data. Auditing this static data for accuracy is a key strategy for success. This is the foundation for the new system. The output is only as good as the inputs.

## Enter Dynamic Data

Most systems will not allow the automatic upload of dynamic data such as purchase orders, open work orders, and accounts payable. Opening these orders and moving them through the process affects many areas of the system, including finance. For best results, these items should be manually input into the database. Transfer onto the new system is an excellent opportunity to clean up these orders.

## Document Policies and Procedures

This last task is the one that unfortunately does not get done effectively. Here's an excellent place to use a college intern. Policies and procedures do not have to be the thickness of *War and Peace*. The best policies and procedures are no more than one page, front and back. The policy statement of what is intended to be accomplished is on the front. The procedural steps to accomplish that objective are detailed in a flowchart format on the back. What could be more simple? This approach is consistent with ISO 9000 and will not bury the plant in paperwork. Experience has shown that these one-page procedures often get posted on the wall or file cabinet for quick reference by their users.

Figure 11–1 is a sample of the process flow procedure. The steps taken in this procedure fit on one piece of paper in flowchart format. This would be the equivalent of a four- to five-page written procedure. Which do you think will be really used?

## Cutover

The whole company is eventually brought onto the new system. The approach of bringing up chunks at a time allows for continuous

**FIGURE  11–1**

Sample Process Flow

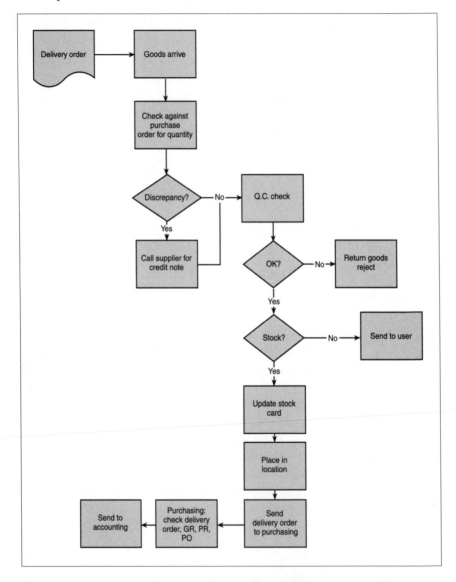

improvement to take place in the utilization of the system during
the implementation. After the whole company has been brought
on line, this is an excellent time to review the performance

measures for the system and determine what positive results have already been made. Return on investment from the early chunks that are implemented should fund the continuation of the project to its full completion. Expected results should include increased customer service, lower inventories, and a reduction in the overall stress level. These benefits allow the business to be more profitable and provide it the ability to grow without additional resources.

## Celebrate

This can be the most important step. The journey has been worthwhile. The whole company has just completed a major project. Celebrating recognizes this accomplishment and clearly demonstrates its importance to the company. This step is frequently forgotten.

## SUMMARY

Selecting and implementing a new manufacturing control system can appear overwhelming. Using a few simple tools, the company can achieve success in a very short time. The most important tool in the implementation toolbox is education. Attempting to implement what is not well understood is very difficult. A common vision of the goal and clear expectations of the outcome including benefits to the company expedite the whole process. When modern MRP systems are carefully examined, 80 to 90 percent of the system is the same; 10 to 20 percent is different and makes the system uniquely fit the company. Expect that the selected system will last for three to five years because changing technology will introduce new tools and increased benefits. The financial benefit of an integrated planning system should be realized within the first 18 months. The largest benefits typically come from reduced inventory, improved cash flow, and improved customer service. These factors combine to allow growth for the company without the addition of overhead resources. This improves the overall profitability and allows for high payoff investments for further growth. Selecting a new system is not a random shot in the dark but, like any new tool, a system must be carefully selected, understood, and applied to support the future of the company.

# 12

## ⊚ BEGINNING THE JOURNEY

### OPENING THE TOOLBOX

Every journey begins with the vision of success. A clear under-standing is required of the destination. As the adage goes, "If we don't know where we are going, any road will get us there." The saying applies to the implementation of integrated business sys-tems. In many companies unsuccessful in this journey, lack of top management support is blamed for system failure. In reality, con-fusion throughout the company is the root cause for not achiev-ing expectations. Clear system objectives and process controls provide the visibility to be successful. Performance measurements and overall company goals must be aligned to achieve overall business success. Only then can the tools be selected that will be successful. Real top management support comes from providing the strategic vision, not from detailed meddling in the imple-mentation minutiae.

The recent resurgence of interest in MRP systems can be directly attributed to two causes. First, the cost of technology declining at an amazing rate makes these sophisticated inte-grated business planning tools affordable for even the smallest company. Second, the pressures of the market to mass customize product and provide at a profit "just what is needed, when it is needed, exactly how the customer wants it" requires a tighter control of the material process than ever before. In general, the length of product life cycles is declining dramatically. Correspondingly, the risk of obsolescence is increasing. Add to this that the highest percentage component of the cost of goods sold is directly attributable to material, and the result is a renewed interest in improving the material control process. Continuous process improvement requires fully understanding the current process and the desired results of that process. Shewhart developed the "plan-do-check-act (PDCA)" cycle to make process improvement clear and understandable. This approach also fits the material process.

MRP is a key tool for improving control of material in any size company. Understanding how a process performs is critical when designing a planning and control system. Controls must be applied in meaningful places to provide an early warning system before the process goes way out of control. The danger of not fully understanding the interrelationships in the manufacturing process before implementing a planning and control system like MRP is that controls will likely be put in the wrong places. Parts of the process really causing problems go unnoticed and uncontrolled while normal variation in other areas gets too much attention.

Successful effective control systems fit the unique production process. Even within the same production facility, different control systems may be necessary for different processes. Attempting to force fit the same control system or production philosophy to all processes in a facility can set the entire system up for failure. Only through a complete understanding of the processes can effective control systems be established. MRP systems have many filters, controls, and reports that can be used to alert the planner when the material process is out of control. The real power of MRP is that it plans by exception and notifies the planner only when action is required.

A typical manufacturing company contains many different types of processes. For example, a company that fabricates and assembles a product has two different manufacturing approaches. Since fabrication usually uses only a few raw material inputs, the process requires that all raw materials are available when the fabrication is scheduled to begin. Usually a fabrication process has higher variability of yields. Yield is the quantity that successfully completes a process. This is typically less than the quantity that begins the process. The loss can be due to parts needed for setup, parts scrapped during the process, or normal attrition of the process.

To ensure that the quantity required in inventory is available, additional raw material is planned through the material requirements planning (MRP) system. These scrap and yield factors can affect all the parts in the bill of material. In that case, the scrap quantity would be placed at the parent level in the item master. Alternatively, possibly only one material is subject to scrap. This scrap factor would be placed in the detailed bill of material relationship. Either way, MRP will plan the appropriate amount of additional inventory to provide sufficient raw materials for the process. In the event that the process has an unreliable scrap factor, safety stock may be used. This helps to ensure that the variability is covered by sufficient inventory to keep the production process going. Remember that addressing variability is one of the functions of inventory covered in Chapter 1. Increasing the reliability of the manufacturing process dramatically decreases the inventory required in the production system.

When the same product reaches the final assembly phase, the production processes are more standardized. Depending on the length and complexity of the assembly process, components can be required at different times during the entire process. Assembly is normally a more predictable process, so safety stock is not required to ensure that the production target will be met. The execution system could be a simple pull system using a daily production rate. The detailed transaction feedback of operation by operation completions to a centralized computer may not be needed. This is common in a highly repetitive process. Since the materials move so quickly through the process, the on-hand is close to zero. MRP is simplified and the master production schedule drives the material plan directly.

Deducting materials after they are used is a possible way to manage component material. This procedure is known as backflushing. Another popular procedure is the picking method. This is used to issue all the materials at once to the shop floor. The choice between these tools depends on the repetitiveness and lead time of the assembly. If an assembly line is building the same product every day or in very small lot sizes, picking all the material to bring it to the line at the beginning of the job takes a significant amount of time and effort, without any accompanying control or value. If the assembly line builds in larger batches, the pick list and movement of all required materials to the line at one time can make good sense. Either way, MRP can be used to plan raw materials and control inventory, but different shop floor control techniques are used.

Remember that MRP is the acronym for material requirements planning. Many people will have you believe that MRP is an old tool that is no longer effective in today's rapidly changing environment. Whatever the processes used in the company, MRP is an excellent planning tool that provides visibility of raw material requirements. This visibility is a key tool for reducing the cost of materials because buyers can provide the future requirements to the suppliers, most likely reducing cost. When you consider that 60 to 70 percent of the cost of goods sold in a modern company is material, the increased profits this can yield for the company can be significant. Many companies pay for the entire MRP implementation through reduced inventory and purchase price reduction.

Effective inventory management should help the company compete in its desired product market. The pace of competition and expectations of customers are increasing exponentially. Many different objectives are cited for manufacturing firms. A few from that long list are to make a profit, maximize shareholder wealth, become world class, win additional market share, survive a poor economy, and provide employment for the family. Whatever the goals of the company, they must be well defined and communicated to all employees. This strategic focus of the company defines the competitive road that all employees should follow. Like taking a car trip, it is very difficult to know if you have arrived when you do not know where you are going.

Regardless of other strategic goals, every company must profitably serve the customer to survive. Some companies have defined their main focus as short lead time response; others have chosen to quickly innovate new product designs and features; still others have pursued a strategy of lowest cost. In the past, management has considered these approaches trade-offs to one another. To be most competitive, one strategy is chosen as the main vision. This is not to say the others can be ignored. Trade-off thinking is dangerous. One item is chosen for a main focus, assuming that the others must suffer. To compete in today's market, a company must meet market acceptance for many things. What is our strategy? Where are we going?

## DEVELOPING THE VISION

The vision for a company is where the leader wants to go. Is the vision to grow to a certain size or stay about the same? The entrepreneurial business executive has a clear vision in mind. To have others help achieve this vision, the first step must be to communicate to every person in the company the vision of how the company will compete and what the goals are. The process of communicating the vision can help clarify it for the executive. Too often, systems are installed that directly conflict with or, at a minimum, get in the way of the long-term goals. This communication does not require a large time investment by top management. An excellent start can be made in less than one day. The questions to be answered include:

What is the philosophy of the company?

What is the strategy of the company, including identification of strengths, weaknesses, opportunities, and threats?

How shall we structure the company to support the strategy?

What things must be accomplished to fulfill the strategy and support the overall vision?

When this company self-examination is completed, the goals and objectives can be clarified by using the following format:

We are _____.

We will _____.

So that _____.

As measured by _____.

When fully thought out, this definition should easily fit on one side of a single sheet of paper, worded so every person in the company can read and understand it. Concise statements clarify the vision and goals for the company. Do not spend time editing every word and comma. This does not add value. The important task is to capture the essence of the company and where it wants to go. Expect that parts of this statement will be a living document that changes as the market changes. Other parts, like the core philosophical beliefs, should stay the same no matter what market and product.

## CREATING THE MISSION STATEMENT

What is the philosophy of the company? What do you think of when you think of your company? Some answers may include being customer focused, always on time, the low-cost producer, and product design innovator. Beware of the desire to try to be everything to everyone. Mission statements have been developed that contain every superlative adjective available, such as "We will be the premier supplier of a full line of product at the lowest price and the shortest lead time at the highest profit. Our number one priority is our customers, our employee safety, and product quality." While each of the items described in the mission statement is important, where is the focus? A clear focus allows a company to be the most successful. These clear goals provide the basis for daily activity.

The company philosophy should be stated in less than six words. David Belasco, the theatrical producer, said, "If you can't write your idea on the back of my calling card, you don't have a clear idea." During the development of wordy mission statements, many hours of work are spent selecting and usually fighting over just the right words, phrases, and punctuation. After one year of having the mission on the front office wall, hardly anyone can remember what it says or why those particular words were so important. In an attempt to keep people connected to the mission statement, a copy is affixed to the back of each employee's identification card. If the mission statement truly provided the daily touchstone, this would not be necessary.

A true mission is one that can be communicated in a few words and is the reference for everyday decisions at the company. A classic case of a clear mission statement is the heavy equipment manufacturer, Komatsu. Its mission was "BEAT CAT," where "CAT" was the Caterpillar company in the United States. What part of that mission could be forgotten or misunderstood? A card attached to each person's ID was not necessary. This philosophy statement was a rallying point for everyone in the company.

The material department at a large equipment plant in Seattle is very clear on its mission. Surprisingly its mission is not low-cost materials or on-time delivery. Its primary focus is "safety first." Employees' everyday actions support this mission as they focus on bringing in material that can be moved safely to the line and can be lifted safely to assemble into their big equipment. A companywide commitment to safety was evident as the new factory was built. Its multiple loading docks around the outside of the plant allow materials to be moved safely to positions on the line without endangering assembly workers.

Nordstrom has become famous for its focus on servicing the customer. Its "no questions asked" return policy assures customers that they need not worry. Sales associates daily go above and beyond the call of normal fashion specialty store expectation to ensure their customers' satisfaction. The result is loyal customers and increased sales. Maytag's vision is to build household appliances that work reliably. Its classic advertisements of the lonely Maytag technician clearly communicate this vision for the company. These companies have a clear vision of the ultimate goals for the organization, not long, wordy mission statements.

Leveraging off the reputation for customer service, a plant in Kent, Washington, had the goal to be the "Nordstrom of manufacturing." This facility was a sole source supplier of one product line for one customer. Keeping this customer happy was essential to keeping the contract. If the customer said a part was bad, the quality department did not argue and show where the specifications were unclear. The part was replaced and the underlying situation was addressed. This total focus on the customer resulted in the company winning the customer's most prestigious supplier award in the first year of business and additional business for the company. The saying that "the customer may not always be right, but they are always the customer" proved true many times. Everyone in the company was aware of the key vision, and it contributed to every decision made.

Care must be taken that although the vision may state one thing, the daily actions of management communicate what is really important. If in the written mission statement retaining skilled employees is the highest value, but every business downturn yields layoffs, the words in the mission statement are meaningless. In total quality management classes, managers are taught to "walk the talk." Shipping substandard product at the end of the month just to make the revenue numbers demonstrates the true focus of the company. Longfellow said: "Your actions speak so loud, I can't hear what you say." The vision and daily actions of the management team must be aligned to effectively communicate the importance to everyone in the company so the desired competitive strategy can be implemented.

Selecting effective performance measures can help align everyone with the desired goals. A common human behavior is that we behave according to how we are measured. If you see behavior that is not acceptable, look at the performance measurement system. Employees who are censured for being late on a time card quickly learn to have someone else punch their card. Now the problem is dishonesty in addition to lateness. Having attentive supervisors or coaches actively participating in the area allows this behavior to be addressed as it happens. Selecting effective performance measures is the most difficult thing senior management must do. These measures, like highway mileposts, provide progress markers on the route toward the vision using the strategy.

## BUILDING THE STRATEGY

What is the strategy of the company? This must reflect the strengths, weaknesses, opportunities, and threats experienced by the company. Each factor is considered in turn as a strategy is developed for the company. Ideally the strategy will capitalize on the strengths, address weaknesses, seize opportunities, and mitigate threats.

## Strengths

Strengths are internal advantages the company has over the competition. Strengths can be long-term, highly skilled employees, talented product design personnel, location of the business, years in business, and so on. Entrepreneurial businesses typically have a flexible multifunctional staff that is very dedicated to the success of the company. The relationship between employees is like a family, whether or not there are true blood relationships. This strength in entrepreneurial business raises employees above and beyond the call of duty on a regular basis because they have a significant emotional if not financial investment in the company. Another strength in small companies is the financial commitment. Usually small enterprises are funded by the personal assets of the founder, who remains an active participant in the business. Depending on the depth of the founder's pocket, this may eliminate the need for loans or credit lines from banks to fund the operations of the company.

Small companies are capable of nimble responses to the market that are not possible in larger companies. Since many people wear multiple hats, the lines of communication are shorter. A large company may have multiple departments containing hundreds of people performing the functions that a handful of people accomplish in the entrepreneurial business. No wonder that the growth area at the end of this decade and into the next century is predicted in the small business sector. The focus on customer service and overall responsiveness favor the capabilities of the small, entrepreneurial business. These strengths, coupled with technological advantages, can be cornerstones for the development of an effective strategy.

## Weaknesses

Weaknesses are internal items that cause the company concern. They may be accidents, high employee turnover, bureaucracy, and so on. One weakness plagues virtually every small company—cash flow. The beneficent founder has a limit to the amount of financial resources available to the company. The company can be extremely profitable, but if cash does not flow in a timely fashion, the business can grind to a painful stop. The effective management of inventory is key to cash management. Having long-term relationships with suppliers with favorable payment terms, coupled with short lead times within the plant, can turn cash flow problems into a worry of the past. Just the process of calculating cash flow can be a weakness for an entrepreneurial business. Unless someone in the company has an understanding of the sources and uses of cash and can offset these factors with timing, generating a cash flow statement can be a nightmare. Usually entrepreneurial businesses are founded by product or market experts, and rarely is there someone in the operation with a good understanding of the financials and their relationship to the daily operation. This can leave the financial analysis sadly neglected until it is too late to recover.

Some of the same strengths of a entrepreneurial business also become weaknesses. The entrepreneurial spirit of the founder and the single provision source for resources can allow this person to change from a benevolent provider to an autocratic dictator. Since his personal finances are on the line, he has a tendency to insist on having things done his way. That same talented design department listed as a strength may also be a weakness because it may be a department of one. Since so many activities are performed by only one person, when that person is missing, the activities often cease. Weaknesses may include an imbalance in the talents of the management team. The management team may be brilliant engineers but not know much about how to manage a business. Many small companies grow to a size only large enough to be managed on the back of an index card because that is all the management team knows how to do. The expectations of growth are different for small enterprises. Having an ultimate goal of $10 million in sales prevents the management team from even considering an opportunity that would propel the company to a $25 million business.

Many founders want a company just large enough to satisfy their appetite for developing new products and to sell the designs and early working prototypes. Other entrepreneurial business owners want only to provide employment for various members of the family. These self-constraints are a weakness in the face of a growing market since the systems will not be developed to support growth. Honest identification of these weaknesses must be included in the development of overall strategy.

## Opportunities

Opportunities are outside the company and provide a possibility for the company to grow and flourish. These opportunities can be:

- Rapidly expanding markets such as high-technology consumer electronics.
- Favorable government regulations, as in the area of recycling and other environment-friendly business.
- Social changes like the baby boomer generation that demand new products such as convenience products, health club services, and sportier cars.

Understanding the market and market opportunities can focus the overall strategy for the firm. Unique opportunities for entrepreneurial businesses are the demands for decreased response time, overall flexibility, and nimbleness. The uniqueness of entrepreneurial business, where everyone usually wears many hats, is that changes in the market can be recognized, addressed, and serviced more quickly. Even though the larger company may have the strength of additional resources, these resources are accompanied by a bureaucratic structure that prevents them from quickly understanding and responding to the needs of the customer. The best understanding of the market can be obtained from talking to customers and potential customers. Many times the management team believes it knows what the customer wants. When the customer is asked, the answers can be surprising. Businesses that can profitably service the needs of the specific customer or micromarket will ensure success for years to come. The best opportunity for entrepreneurial business is to address micromarkets or niches. These markets have different expectations and demands that can be serviced best by the uniquely responsive entrepreneurial business. In addition, these markets usually offer higher profit margins than the standard price-sensitive market.

## Threats

Threats are external events or conditions that jeopardize the firm's profitability, growth, or existence. Government regulations, weather, union strikes, market shifts, and new competitors could adversely affect the company. A company that addresses the changing needs of the market can keep ahead of threats such as changes in technology. Gas-guzzler cars severely hurt U.S. auto makers when the companies failed to recognize the threat posed by the market shift to better fuel efficiency. Computer manufacturers face the ever present threat of technology changes and managing the upgrade of machines. With the improved power of personal computers and the development of microcomputers, the need for large mainframes with hardware-specific applications has been significantly reduced. Small companies fear the presence of larger companies entering their market with all their resources and sophisticated marketing techniques. Entrepreneurial business strategy must clearly identify and address market expectations and how they can best service them.

## STRATEGIC PLAN FOCUS

The strategic plan should capitalize on the strengths to overcome the weaknesses in order to capitalize on the opportunities while mitigating the threats. Sounds a little like walking a tightrope, doesn't it? Every company must profitably serve the customer to survive. Some companies have defined their main focus as short lead time response; others have chosen to quickly innovate new product designs and features; still others have pursued a strategy of lowest cost. In the past, management has considered these approaches trade-offs to one another. To be most competitive, one strategy is chosen as the main focus. This is not to say the others can be ignored. To compete in tomorrow's market, a company must meet market levels of acceptance for many things. However, a main focus must be chosen for excellence and be consistent with the overall philosophy and vision of the company. Just as in the opportunities and threat identification, knowing what the market demands and expects is essential for developing strategy. Three factors need to be considered: order winners, order qualifiers, and nonissues.

## Order Winners

Order winners are competitive issues that cause a customer to buy from a particular company. These can be very different for individual customers, but usually each market niche group exhibits similar characteristics. In the case of personal computers, the order winners may be preloaded software included in the price of the machine. For the Saturn car company, aggressive pursuit of the market segment that desires a hassle-free experience when buying and owning a car has proven to be an order winner. Order winners can be low price, rapid delivery speed, high delivery reliability, leading edge product design, flexibility, excellent after-market service, desirable image, or exceptional quality. Obviously companies cannot be the world's best at all of these. Only one or two items are selected for concentration as a core competence. Nordstrom clearly sells image and aftermarket service with its exceptional reputation for customer service. Stories are told of items being returned to Nordstrom for a credit that were not even purchased there. Maytag does not use low price as a competitive edge. It targets the market segment that likes appliances that work, first time, every time. It charges a premium price for its products in a very price-sensitive market. Automotive marketing techniques show many different types of order-winner strategies. Kia competes on low price for a "well-made car." Lexus and Infiniti compete on image and quality. Saturn sells uncompromising service and a high-value, low-cost car. Porsche and Ferrari compete in an entirely different market segment. The selected order-winning strategies must answer the needs of the target market.

## Order Qualifiers

Order winners are the items that can tip the scales in your company's favor once the order qualifiers are met. In the 1970s, quality was an order winner. This characteristic has now become an order qualifier. Order qualifiers are items that are expected just to be in the game. The same list of order winners—price, delivery speed, delivery reliability, product design, flexibility, aftermarket service, image, and quality—may be on the order qualifier list, depending on the market. The quality of American automobiles was given an overhaul during the 1980s after the Americans stopped buying the big, poorly made U.S. cars and started buying small, well-made cars from Japan. Today, car makers must have high-quality cars just to qualify for a buyer's consideration. The increase in warranty for a new car from one year to three years supports this commitment and improvement in quality.

Attempting to charge a premium price for a product or service that is in the commodity market will guarantee failure. Airline companies are scrambling to address the order qualifiers and order winners of their market. In-flight services have been dropped in an effort to reduce air fares, the identified order qualifier. When an airline with full service has the same price ticket as the cut-rate airline, clearly the order is won by the full-service airline. When there is a significant difference in price, some customers may be willing to endure the inconveniences and crowded conditions of the cut-rate airlines to save money. Cut-rate airlines have attempted to compete not just with other airlines but with other modes of transportation like trains and busses. This strategy has been very successful for their market niche of infrequent fliers with plenty of time. Business travelers quickly tire of the crowded conditions and the need to check in at multiple lines to check baggage and then pick up boarding passes. The boarding process is extremely stressful where everyone fights for numerical place in line to claim a preferred seat. The order qualifiers for the business traveler can be very different from the order qualifier for the casual traveler. A small difference in air fare will not dissuade frequent business travelers from their preferred assigned seats, frequent flier miles, and an orderly boarding process. Understanding the needs and wants of the potential customer is essential in the identification of order qualifiers.

## Nonissues

Nonissues are items about which the customer just does not care. Interestingly, they can be the same list as the order winners and order qualifiers—price, delivery speed, delivery reliability, product design, flexibility, aftermarket service, image, and quality. Even though advertisers may attempt to segment the market based on these items, the customer does not really care. For example, bathroom tissue does not sell based on aftermarket service or flexibility. Understanding and not spending limited resources on non-issues can be a critical success factor for the company. Hotels spend resources folding the toilet tissue to a point. Does this service cause a customer to choose that hotel? Why do so many insist on performing this task? Careful consideration must be given to those tasks considered important by the company but are nonissues for the customer.

## STRATEGY STATEMENT

The overall strategy of the company must identify and acknowledge order winners, order qualifiers, and nonissues in the light of the overall philosophy, strengths, weaknesses, opportunities, and threats. A clear summary of each of the building blocks helps focus the strategy statement. The company examines the market needs and determines what is helping to satisfy those needs. More important is the identification of what is preventing satisfaction of those needs. This gap analysis should result in a list of items prioritized by the level to which they prevent the company from achieving its vision. Many gap items may impact each other. Examining the list to determine the root causes helps prioritize action to take. Use "if-then" statements to connect the gap items to each other. The items left at the base of this interrelationship are the root cause issues that must be addressed. The strategy statement clearly defines what action will be done. Each action should tie directly back to the overall vision and philosophy. Now that the "what" has been determined, the focus turns to "who."

## ORGANIZATIONAL STRUCTURE

Effective planning and control systems help move a company from the fire fighting mode to what real fire fighting professionals actually do with most of their time—fire prevention. Developing an organizational structure to support the intended strategy should help improve the competitive position of the company. If the strategy is to compete in a market where the order winners and qualifiers are rapid response and excellent customer service, having a relatively flat organization with an enabled, empowered workforce would help accomplish this goal. If low cost were the overall strategy, having a centralized organization with a standard product to take advantage of the economies of scale would support the goals. The organizational structure can be considered the roads that are laid down for vehicles to travel on. The mission identifies the final destination for the journey, the strategy defines the method of transportation like roads, and the organizational structure determines the layout of the roads and the exact traffic patterns. Laying a superhighway to an undesired destination or meandering around the countryside to get to your final destination is a terrible waste of critical resources.

Developing a hierarchical infrastructure in a company that competes by quick response to the market puts a stranglehold on the company's vitality. To use the Nordstrom example again, its exemplary customer service is possible because each employee has been empowered to make decisions on the spot about how to best service the customer. A supervisor or manager does not need to be called to make many decisions. This empowerment is possible due to effective training and education provided to each employee. UPS has a unique approach to organizational structure. Each manager or supervisor has had to ascend through the ranks of the package loader or truck washer. This provides a cohesive workforce that fully understands how decisions on one level affect other levels in the organization.

The number of levels of the organization's hierarchy and the reporting relationships within that structure can directly affect the overall company's performance. Closely linking the "what" of the strategic vision to the "who" of the organizational structure can result in a competitive edge for the company.

## TACTICAL TOOLS

Finally, the cars can be put on the road to business success. Effective planning enhances smooth execution. Imagine trying to reach a destination where there are no roads and no map. Many companies attempt to do this every day in the competitive arena and fail. Now, after all the top-level planning, tactics can be developed for implementing a successful strategy. Integrating the needs of the market with the overall production plan and tactics of the company enhances overall company success.

The tools and techniques described in previous chapters are some tactical actions and tools that will move a company toward its vision. Inventory is a critical investment for entrepreneurial businesses. These tools will improve the overall financial results when skillfully used. This is why so much attention is spent on defining and implementing planning and control systems as part of the company's tactics. Attempting to fit the same control system or production philosophy to all processes in a facility can set up the entire system for failure. There is a large box of tools available for use. Only through a complete understanding of the processes and available tools can effective control systems be established.

## SUMMARY

Clearly defined and understood vision, philosophy, strategy, structure, and tactics allow the people in the company to use the tools in their toolbox for maximum success. Valuable time is spent on high-return activities. Each person has a clear understanding of the company's direction and how he is an integral part of its success.

There are a myriad of technologies and systems a company can choose from to ease the workload of managing a business. Companies that have successfully implemented MRP systems find that their material management function is very responsive and makes excellent use of their inventory investment. World-class implementations take no more time or resources than ineffective ones. The difference has been shown to be where the efforts are placed. World-class companies invest their efforts in education and training and follow the described proven implementation path. Companies with ineffective results generally jump in full speed, not knowing where they are going. They make a big splash but achieve little else.

According to a Chinese proverb, "The journey of a thousand miles begins with a single step." Developing a strategic plan is making that first step. Open your toolbox and fill it with the correct set of hand tools, power tools, and the knowledge of how to use them. This successful combination enables you and your company to experience optimum results along your journey.

Remember to enjoy the trip!

# REFERENCES

APICS, *8th Edition Dictionary*. Falls Church, VA: APICS, 1995.

Arnold, J. R. Tony. *Introduction to Materials Management*, Englewood Cliffs, NJ: Prentice–Hall, 1991.

Goldratt, Eli. *The Goal*, Croton-on-Hudson, NY: North River Press, 1986.

Lareau, William. *American Samurai*, New York, NY: Warner Books, 1991.

Orlicky, Joseph. *MRP: Materials Requirements Planning: The New Way of Life in Production and Inventory Management*, New York, NY: McGraw–Hill Book Company, 1975.

Plossl, George. *Orlicky's Material Requirements Planning*, 2nd edition, New York, NY: McGraw Hill, Inc., 1994.

Schonberger, Richard. *World Class Manufacturing: The Lessons of Simplicity Applied*, NY: Free Press, 1986.

# INDEX

🌀